ADMONITION FOR NEGLECTFUL

ADMONITION FOR THE NEGLECTFUL

Tanmbihul Ghafellen

Faqih Abu Lais Samarqandi (A.R)

Adam Publishers & Distributors

ADAM PUBLISHERS & DISTRIBUTORS
Exporters & Importers
1542, Pataudi House, Darya Ganj,
New Delhi-110002
Phone (O) : 23271690, 23282550
Fax: 23267510 (R) 95120- 2553953

e-mail:apd@bol.net. in
www.adambooks.com

© **Publishers**

Edition - 2004

ISBN : 81-7435-313-5

Printed & Bound in India Published by
S. Sajid Ali for
ADAM PUBLISHERS & DISTRIBUTORS
1542, Pataudi House, Darya Ganj,
New Delhi-110002

ADMONITION FOR THE NEGLECTFUL

INDEX

ADMONITION FOR THE NEGLECTFUL 1
FORWARD 17
ADMONITION FOR THE NEGLECTFUL.................19
1. SINCERITY .
OSTENTATION IS A MINOR FORM OF POLYTHEISM. 19
THE SIMILITUDE OF OSTENTATION.................19
SEVEN THINGS ARE WORTHLESS WITHOUT SEVEN THINGS.....19
A DOUBLE REWARD FOR AN ACTION COMING TO THE FORE. ...20
WHO ARE THE SINCERE ONES?....................21
RECOGNIZING THE CHOSEN SERVANTS
OF ALLAAH : - FOUR TRAITS.....................21
FOUR SIGNS OF OSTENTATION. 21
THE FORT FOR ACTIONS. 21
LEARN SINCERITY FROM A SHEPHERD. 22
FOUR CONDITIONS FOR THE ACCEPTANCE OF ACTIONS.22
HOW TO RECOGNIZE PIETY :- THREE FACTORS............22
THREE IMPORTANT FACTORS. 23
THREE FACTORS CAUSE DESTRUCTION.................23
THE FOUR NAMES OF A BOASTFUL PERSON. 24
THE SIMILITUDE OF GOOD ACTIONS. 24
AN INCIDENT.................25
2. DEATH AND IT'S SEVERITY.
THE PANGS OF DEATH ARE A WORD OF CAUTION..........25
APPRECIATING FIVE THINGS BEFORE FIVE. 25
WINTER IS A BLESSING FOR THE MU'MIN. 26
THE GRAVE IS EITHER A GARDEN
OF JANNAH OR A PIT OF JAHANNAM. 26
THE SIMILITUDE OF DEATH. 26
THREE THINGS SHOULD NOT BE FORGOTTEN. 27
ONLY FOUR PERSONS APPRECIATE FOUR THINGS..........27
THE REALITY OF DEATH. 27
WHEN ACTIONS CONTRADICT WORDS :- 4 THINGS.......28
THREE THINGS ARE ASTONISHING.................28
DEATH DOES NOT ALLOW FATNESS. 29
**THE CONSEQUENCE OF REMEMBERING DEATH
AND OF NOT REMEMBERING**
DEATH :- 3 BOUNTIES / 3 PUNISHMENTS.................29

THE TASTE OF DEATH IS EXTREMELY BITTER. 29
FOUR IMPORTANT FACTORS. 30
THE FOUR SIGNS OF A PERSON WHO
AWAKENS FROM HIS NEGLIGENCE. 30
THE BEST PERSON :- 5 TRAITS. 31
THREE NOBLE QUALITIES. 31
THE BEST AND MOST INTELLIGENT PERSON. 31
3. PUNISHMENT IN THE GRAVE.
FIVE TYPES OF GLAD TIDINGS. 32
EIGHT THINGS THAT WILL SAVE ONE FROM
THE PUNISHMENT OF THE GRAVE. 33
ALLAAH DETESTS FOUR THINGS IN PARTICULAR. 33
A GOLDEN SAYING. 34
A STARTLING INCIDENT. 34
THE ANNOUNCEMENTS OF THE EARTH:- 5 CALLS. 34
AN ALARMING INCIDENT. 35
THE SCREAMS OF THE DEAD..35
4. THE SCENES OF QIYAAMAT.
THE TREES OF JANNAH. 43
ONE OF THE DAMSELS OF JANNAH CALLED LA'IBA.........44
TH E BEAUTY OF THE PEOPLE OF JANNAH. 44
THE GREATEST BOUNTY OF JANNAH. 44
HADHRAT JIBREEL (A.S) APPEARS IN A STRANGE
MANNER TO CONVEY GLAD TIDINGS. 45
THERE WILL BE NO NEED TO RELIEVE ONESELF IN JANNAH...46
A TREE IN JANNAH CALLED "TOOBA." 47
THE APPEARANCE OF JANNAH. 47
FIVE CONDITIONS FOR ADMISSION INTO JANNAH.........48
WORDS OF WISDOM :- 3 FACTS. 49
THE STORY OF AN ASCETIC. 49
A STORY OF HADHRAT IBRAHEEM BIN ADHAM (R.A). 49
FOOD FOR THOUGHT. 50
A STATEMENT OF HADHRAT ABU HAAZIM (R.A). 50
THE DOWRY FOR JANNAH..50
THE INTERCESSION OF JANNAH AND JAHANNAM..........50
THE BAZAARS OF JANNAH. 51
WHO IS THERE WHO DESIRES JANNAH?.......................51
5. THE MERCY OF ALLAAH.
THE HOPE AND PRAYERS OF HADHRAT YAHYA BIN
MU'AADH RAAZI (R.A):- 3 DUAAS................................52
NEVER MAKE ANYONE DESPONDENT OF ALLAAH'S MERCY. .53
AN OATH MAY BE TAKEN ON FOUR THINGS. 53
INTERCESSION WILL BE ON BEHALF OF THE SINNERS.......53

A THOUGHT PROVOKING INCIDENT. 54
GLAD TIDINGS..55
GOLDEN WORDS. 55
A STUNNING INCIDENT ABOUT ALLAAH'S FORGIVENESS. ...55
CONCISE ADVICE. 56
SEVEN CATEGORIES OF PEOPLE WILL BE SHADED
BENEATH THE THRONE OF ALLAAH. 56
*6. ENJOINING WHAT IS RIGHT AND FORBIDDING WHAT
IS EVIL.*
GLAD TIDINGS..57
RECOGNIZING A MU'MIN AND A HYPOCRITE. 57
A REMARK BY HADHRAT ALI (R.A). 58
A TECHNIQUE IS REQUIRED WHEN ENJOINING GOOD....58
TYRANNICAL RULERS ARE THE RESULT OF FAILURE TO.......58
ENJOIN GOOD AND FORBID EVIL.....................................58
THE CATEGORIES OF ENJOINING GOOD AND
FORBIDDING EVIL. 59
A FASCINATING STORY..59
FIVE CONDITIONS FOR A PREACHER..............................60
7. REPENTANCE
THE BEHAVIOR OF MAN IS STRANGE INDEED................61
TAUBA IS ACCEPTED ONLY BEFORE DEATH. 62
THE REMORSE AND DESPONDENCY OF THE ACCURSED
IBLEES :- IN FIVES..62
SIX QUALITIES OF ONE WHO TRULY RECOGNIZES Allaah. ...62
THE EMINENT FUDAIL (R.A). 63
TAUBATUN NASOOHA
(SINCERE REPENTANCE):-3 SIGNS. 64
THE RESOLUTION NOT TO REPEAT A SIN IS IMPERATIVE
WHEN ONE REPENTS. 64
A UNIQUE STORY..64
HASTE IS BEST IN THREE THINGS. 65
THE SIGNS OF TAUBA. 65
FOUR HONOR THAT ALLAAH CONFERS UPON ONE WHO
REPENTS..66
THE FIRE OF JAHANNAM WILL NOT AFFECT THE
REPENTANT PERSON AS HE CROSSES OVER IT. 67
THE WARNING AGAINST TAUNTING A MUSLIM. 67
SINS ARE TOTALLY OBLITERATED BY TAUBA. 67

THE EXCELLENCE OF THE UMMAH OF Rasulullaah (sallAllaahu-
alaihi-wasallam)..67
GOOD ACTIONS ARE AWAITED BEFORE A SIN IS RECORDED:-
5 SINS...68
SINS ARE TRANSFORMED INTO GOOD ACTIONS BY
VIRTUE OF TAUBA. 69
THE STATEMENT OF HADHRAT MOOSA (A.S). 70
THE REPENTANCE OF ZAAZAAN.....................................70
A THOUGHT PROVOKING INCIDENT. 71
A HADITH QUDSI:- 9 ADVICES..72

SERVING ONE'S PARENTS IS SUPERIOR THAN JIHAAD. ..73
THREE ACTIONS ARE NOT ACCEPTED
WITHOUT ANOTHER THREE. 74
DISPLEASING ONE'S PARENTS RESULTS IN A BAD DEATH. 74
CHILDREN OWE TEN RIGHTS TO THEIR PARENTS. 76
PLEASING THE PARENTS AFTER THEIR DEATH:- BY 3 THINGS.76
PARENTS OWE THREE RIGHTS TO THEIR CHILDREN........77
THE CONSEQUENCE OF NOT TEACHING
CHILDRENGOODMANNERS..77
AS YOU SOW, SO SHALL YOU REAP. 78
PERFECT POLITENESS :- REAPS 8 BENEFITS. 78
THE FOUR SIGNS OF GOOD FORTUNE. 78
THE REWARDS OF FIVE THINGS WILL CONTINUE TO
 BE RECEIVED EVEN AFTER DEATH. 79
SOME AHADEETH. 79
8. FOSTERING GOOD RELATIONSHIPS.
THREE QUALITIES OF THE PEOPLE OF JANNAH..............80
A STATEMENT OF HADHRAT UMAR (R.A)......................80
MUSLIMS AND KUFFAR ARE TO BE TREATED
EQUALLY IN THREE RESPECTS....................................80
A STATEMENT OF HADHRAT HASAN BASRI (R.A)...........80
TEN BENEFITS OF FOSTERING GOOD FAMILY RELATIONS....81
THREE GROUPS OF PEOPLE WILL BE BENEATH THE
SHADE OF ALLAAH'S THRONE ON THE DAY OF QIYAMAH.81
ALLAAH LOVES TWO FOOTSTEPS...............................82
FIVE FACTORS THAT INFLATE THE REWARDS OF ACTIONS
TO THE SIZE OF MOUNTAINS AND INCREASES ONE'S
SUSTENANCE..82
SOME AHADEETH. 82
9. RIGHTS OF NEIGHBOURS.
7 TYPES OF PEOPLE UPON WHOM THERE IS NO MERCY. .83
9 RIGHTS ON A NEIGHBOUR..83
5 WORDS OF WISDOM. 84

THREE TYPES OF NEIGHBOURS. 84
THREE ADVICES...85
A FEW PEARLS OF WISDOM. 85
THE POSITION OF A NEIGHBOUR. 85
THREE PRAISEWORTHY TRAITS DURING THE PERIOD OF
IGNORANCE. 86
THE POOR NEIGHBOUR WILL CALL THE RICH NEIGHBOUR
TO TASK..86
TEN OPPRESSORS. 87
FOUR WAYS WHEREBY GOOD RELATIONS MAY BE MAINTAINED
WITH ONE'S NEIGHBOUR. 87
10. LYING.
A SAYING OF HADHRAT LUQMAAN (A.S).......................88
SIX THINGS GUARANTEE JANNAH..................................88

11. BACKBITING.
THE STENCH OF BACKBITING CANNOT BE SMELT WHEN
IT BECOMES HABITUAL. 90
A GIFT IN RETURN FOR EVIL. 90
A SAYING OF HADHRAT IBRAHEEM BIN ADHAM (R.A). ...90
THREE THINGS DESTROY GOOD ACTIONS. 91
THREE THINGS ARE DISTANT FROM MERCY. 91
THREE QUALITIES OF THE PIOUS..............................91
THE ATTITUDE OF THE ANGELS TOWARDS BACKBITING.92
WORDS OF WISDOM DO 3 IF YOU CANNOT DO 3. 92
12. SLANDER
WHO IS THE WORST PERSON? 92
PUNISHMENT IN THE GRAVE FOR THOSE
WHO CARRY TALES:- 3 CAUSES...................................93
CARRYING TALES AND SPREADING ANARCHY. 93
THE PERSON WHO CARRIES TALES IS WORSE THAN THE
DEVIL AND ONE WHO DABBLES IN BLACK MAGIC. 93
SEVEN QUESTIONS. 94
A TALE CARRIER SHOULD NOT BE RELIED ON. 94
CARRYING TALES FORBIDS PRAYERS FROM BEING ACCEPTED. 95
GEMS FROM THE LIPS OF THE PIOUS. 95
13. JEALOUSY
6 THINGS TO DO WHEN SPOKEN ILL OFF....................96
SOME AHADEETH...96
THE ABOMINATION OF JEALOUSY AND MALICE
AND HOW TO REFRAIN FROM THESE. 97
A SUPPLICATION. 97

THE EFFECT OF JEALOUSY FIRST BEFALLS THE JEALOUS
PERSON :- 5 PUNISHMENTS OF JEALOUSY. 98
THE JEALOUS PERSON IS AN ENEMY OF ALLAAH'S BOUNTIES..98
THE RELIGIOUS SCHOLARS ARE MOST GUILTY OF JEALOUSY
SIX THINGS THAT WILL CONDEMN SIX PEOPLE TO............98
JAHANNAM BEFORE RECKONING. 99
A SAYING:- 6 ADVICES...99
JEALOUSY CANNOT BE HARBOURED FOR ANYONE:-
2 REASONS..99
THE ADVICE OF RASULULLAAH (SALLIALLAAHU-ALAIHI-
WASALLAM)
....99
THE JEALOUS PERSON OPPOSES ALLAAH IN 5 WAYS.......100
PRIDE MEANS TO CONSIDER ONESELF AS BEING
SUPERIOR AND TO LOOK DOWN ON OTHERS..............101
14. PRIDE.
THREE PEOPLE ARE DESERVING OF PUNISHMENT........101
THE FIRST THREE PEOPLE TO ENTER JANNAH AND JAHANNAM. 101
ALLAAH DETESTS THREE PERSONS............................102

THE THREE PERSONS WHO ARE MOST BELOVED TO ALLAAH....102
THE REALITY OF PRIDE. 102
THE MOST DETESTABLE PERSON. 103
WORDS OF WISDOM...103
ALLAAH DISLIKES STRUTTING. 103
GOOD CHARACTER MEANS TO BEHAVE HUMBLY
TOWARDS THE HUMBLE AND BEHAVE PROUDLY WITH
THE PROUD. 104
THE HIGHEST FORM OF HUMILITY. 104
HUMILITY IS A TRAIT OF THE AMBIYAA (A.S), WHILE
PRIDE IS THE TRAIT OF THE KUFFAAR. 104
THE HUMILITY OF HADHRAT IBN UMAR (R.A). 105
THE HUMILITY OF HADHRAT UMAR (R.A) 105
THE HUMILITY OF HADHRAT SALMAAN FAARSI (R.A)....106
THE HUMILITY OF HADHRAT ALI (R.A).......................106
RANKS ARE RAISED BY SPENDING IN CHARITY AND BY
FORGIVING OTHERS WITHOUT 3 TRAITS GRANTS JANNAH.107
15. ANGER.
IT IS INCORRECT TO PUNISH ANYONE TO GRATIFY ONESELF.107
ALLAAH LOVES THAT ONE FORGIVES ANOTHER. 107
THE SWEETNESS OF IMAAN IS NOT TASTED
WITHOUT THREE TRAITS. 108
AN INCIDENT OF HOW SHAYTAAN IS INFURIATED. 108
AN ASTONISHING INCIDENT OF HOW SHAYTAAN
DEVIATED PEOPLE:- 3 METHODS. 108

HADHRAT MOOSA (A.S) AND IBLEES :-3 CONDITIONS
IN WHICH ONE SHOULD BE WARY OF SHAYTHAAN.......110
THE ADVICE OF HADHRAT LUQMAAN (A.S):-
RECOGNISE 3 ON 3 OCCASION. 110
AN INCIDENT OF A TAABI'EE (R.A) :- 111
3 QUALITIES OF ONE WORTHY OF PRAISE 111
3 QUALITIES OF JAMATIES 111
3 ADVICES FROM ALLAAH 111
THE ASSISTANCE OF THE ANGELS UPON THE PATIENCE
OF THE OPPRESSED: - 3 ACTS RESULT IN 3 OTHERS. ..112
CONCISE WISDOMS. 112
THE FOUR TYPES OF ASCETICISM.............................113
THE 5 ADVICE OF HADHRAT ABU DARDAA (R.A)..........113
THE TEST OF STRENGTH. 114
DO NOT CURSE AN OPPRESSOR. 114
THE DEFINITION OF HUMANE BEHAVIOUR :-4 ADVICES, ..114
3 BENEFITS OF PATIENCE, 3 HARMS OF HASTE 114
16. THE TONGUE.
FOUR QUALITIES OF A BELIEVER...............................115
A LOFTY POSITION OBTAINED BY 3 QUALITIES. 115
THE STATEMENT OF FOUR KINGS................................116

RECKONING IS EASIER IN THIS WORLD. 116
THE SAINT THAT NEVER SPOKE A WRONG WORD FOR
TWENTY YEARS. 116
SIX SIGNS OF AN IGNORAMUS. 117
A STATEMENT OF HADHRAT ISA (A.S) 8 ADVICES. 117
THE ABOMINATION OF EXCESSIVE LAUGHTER AND 2
HABITS OF THE IGNORANT.........................118
THE ADVICE OF RASULULLAAH
(sallAllaahu-alaihi-wasallam). 119
FOUR ADVICE OF HADHRAT KHIDR (A.S). 119
5A PERSON SHOULD NEVER LAUGH LOUDLY. 119
A SAYING OF HADHRAT HASAN BASRI (R.A)..............120
FOUR FACTORS PREVENT LAUGHTER. 120
THREE THINGS HARDEN THE HEART. 120
LAUGHING AND MAKING OTHERS LAUGH
LEADS TO DESTRUCTION...........................121
BENEFICIAL ADVICE, ...121
5 ADVICES OF RASULULLAAH (S.A.W). 121
8 ADVICES OF HADHRAT UMAR (R.A) 121
8 HARMS OF LAUGHING EXCESSIVELY.....................122
END OF PART ONE.

RAWDATUS SAALIHEEN.

THE IMPRESSIONS OF SOME NOTABLE ULEMA.

HADHRAT MAULANA QAARI TAYYAB SAHEB (A.R) – RECTOR OF DAARUL ULOOM DEOBAND.

We praise Allah and convey salutations to Rasulullah (sallallahu-alayhi-wa-sallam).

A graduate of Daaru Uloom Deoband, Maulana Mahfoozul Hasan, has translated the book, Tambeehul Ghaafileen, written by Faqeeh Abul Laith Samarqandi (A.R), the great scholar of divine sciences.

This humble servant has paged through the book in your hands and derived great benefit from it. A summary of this book is that it is a treasure of gold and gems. It is a wealth of good practices and noble character that will easily make a person ascetic and pious if he keeps this book with him and studies it carefully.

Maulana has favoured the Muslims by placing this fortune in their hands, the worth of which the entire world cannot pay. May Allah grant him the best of rewards. May Allah increase the deeds and knowledge of the translator, perpetuate his grace, and grant the Muslim ummah the ability to derive benefit from him. Aameen.

Muhammed Tayyab (May Allah for give him)
Rector of Daarul Uloom Deoband
16 Dhul Qa'dah 1398 A.H.

HADHRAT MAULANA SAYYID FAKHRUL HASAN SAHEB – SENIOR LECTURER OF DAARUL ULOOM DEOBAND.

I have browsed through the book, Rawdatus Saaliheen, by the respected Maulana Mahfoozul Hasan. This book is actually a translation of the book, Tambeehul Ghaafileen.

I know Maulana from childhood, who is a highly capable graduate of Daarul Uloom Debnand. I agree with the impressions of Maulana Akhlaaq Husain Qaasimi and Mufti Azeezur Rahmaan Bijnoori. However, I personally feel that the book falls short of shedding proper light on the metaphorical beauties of the original.

May Allah bless this work with His acceptance and grant the writer and myself the ability to make further contributions to the Islamic literature. Aameen.

Sayyid Fakhrul Hasan (May Allah forgive him)
Senior lecturer
Daarul Uloom Deoband.

16 Dhul Qa'dah 1398 A.H.

*HADHRAT MAULANA IKHLAAQ HUSAIN
QAASIMI – COMMENTATOR OF THE QUR'AAN
AND CHAIRMAN OF JAMI'ATUL ULEMA DELHI.*

One of the most successful methods of propagating the truth is "maw'izatul hasanah.' The Qur'aan has accorded this method second position of priority amongst three methods. [Surah Nahl, verse 35]

The meaning of "maw'izatul hasanah' is to advise people using effective and captivating methods with the best explanation. It includes instilling Imaan and the fervour to act, using warnings, hopes, similitudes and parables.

The author of this book, Faqeeh Abul Laith Samarqandi (A.R), is renowned for his ability to effectively employ "maw'izatul hasanah.' Hadhrat Maulana Mahfoozul Hasan Qaasimi Sambali (a luminary from a famous family of leading scholars) has successfully captured the effect of this book in this condensed volume.

May Allah accept the efforts of Maulana and create spiritual awareness from this book.

Akhlaaq Husain Qaasimi
Idaara Rahmate Aalam-Delhi
27 September 1978.

FORWARD BY MUFTI AZEEZUR RAHMAAN.

We praise Allah and send salutations to Rasulullah (sallallahu-alayhi-wa-sallam). The book in your hands is a translation of a work titled Tambeehul Ghaafileen, which is famous amongst the ulema. The author of this book was Nasr bin Muhammed bin Ahmed bin Ibraheem, who is better known as Faqeeh Abul Laith Samarqandi (A.R) {who passed away 373 years after the Hijrah}.

Faqeeh Abul Laith Samarqandi (A.R) penned many books containing his fataawa, and is the author of at least fourteen or fifteen works. He was known as Imaamul Huda (the leader of guidance) during his time. He was so pious and particular that he used to take lumps of sand along with him on journeys, to be used to clean after relieving himself. When he was asked about the reason, he replied that he did not like to use the sand of another person without permission.

He used to say that he never spoke a lie since he reached an understanding age. He passed away on the 11th of Jumaadal Ukhra, 373 A.H. A study of conditions in Samarqand and Bukhaara during that period reveals that the ulema concentrated their lectures and public addresses towards spiritual reformation. This fact is also revealed by a study of the lives of people like Hakeem Tirmidhi (A.R), Abu Bakr, Muhammed Is'haaq (A.R) and Faqeeh Abul Laith Samarqandi (A.R). a perusal of books like Tambeehul Ghaafileen, Bustaan and others will portray the same fact.

I have a hand-written copy of Bustaan, which is also penned by Faqeeh Abul Laith Samarqandi (A.R). I have published a translation and commentary of this book, adding references and sources where necessary. After reading Tambeehul Ghaafileen, I intended to translate it as well, but every person cannot do everything. This privilege went to Hadhrat Maulana Mahfoozul Hasan Sambali, who translated the work in a concise form.

How is this book? This is revealed by the historical origin of the book. It is a unique prescription consisting of a blend of subtle advices, words of wisdom, Ahadeeth of Rasulullah (sallallahu-alayhi-wa-sallam) and Qur'aanic verses.

The translator, Maulana Mahfoozul Hasan is an extremely capable youngster, with an eye for intricacies. He is a graduate of Daarul Uloom Deoband. I have read his book from cover to cover. It is excellent. May

Allah accept it. Aameen.

Azeezur Rahmaan (May Allah forgive him)

Madani Daarul Iftaa

Madrasah Madeenatul Uloom

Bijnoor

15 Shawwaal 1398 A.H.

FOREWARD.

The fact cannot be refuted that, just as knowledge is foundational support of actions, a study of the lives of our pious predecessors is one of the most effective ways of spurring actions.

As someone said, "The person who ignores the lives and advices of the pious predecessors is contaminated between two evils. Either he carries out a negligible amount of deeds and considers himself to be amongst the pious predecessors, or he considers his little effort to be extremely great, thereby succumbing to pride and boastfulness. He will then regard himself as the greatest and look down on all others. His efforts will then be worthless and his deeds will be destroyed.

Rasulullah (sallallahu-alayhi-wa-sallam) said, "Meditation for a moment is better than a hundred years of worship." This is the basis of this work.

Since people are inclined towards brevity these days, the lengthy discussions have been omitted, and most of the quotations have been translated in a concise manner.

I am well aware of my deficiencies in knowledge, and I accept that I am unable to do justice to a noble task like translation. However, I long felt the desire in my heart to render a religious service to the public, so that it becomes a means of securing my salvation in the Hereafter. May Allah make this objective be realised.

"This is not difficult for Allah."

There is a great possibility that errors may have occurred in this publication because of my deficient knowledge. I humbly request religious scholars to grace me with a notification of such errors. This is the first part of this series. May Allah grant me the ability and capability to complete the series. Aameen. I plead to the readers not to forget this lowly writer in their du'aas.

NOTE: References have not been given because the author's name carries sufficient weight.

Mahfoozul Hasan Sambali
15 Rabee'uth Thaani 1398 A.H. – 25 March 1978FOREWARD

The original book is in Arabic called "Tambhi ul Gafileen" by Faqih Abu Lais Samarqandi (A.R) A high ranking Faqih(expert on Islaamic Law) and an exemplary par excellence Sufi.

The Urdu translation was done by Moulana Mahfoozul Hassan Sambali entitled "Rawazud Saaliheen".

Numerous commentaries are written on the pearls of wisdom of Faqih Abu Lais (A .R)

We have presented a translation for every Muslim who is interested in strengthening ones Imaan, and improving ones character, personality and behaviour, beautiful guidelines have been provided in this wonderful masterpiece.

Many Sufi scholars use it for their mureeds(disciples) spiritual upbringing.

Because it is so well divided and subdivided, extracts can be easily used as article fillers, page and cover fillers.

Moreover, a book "Thought of the Day" can be gleaned from this book.

Furthermore, extracts can be taken by academic lectures and substantiated by Quraan, Sunnat, statements and actions of Sahabah (R. A) to constitute valuable 'bayaans' (lectures).

We pray that Allaah Taala accepts our efforts to translate into the English language reliable, authentic, valuable material of the Ahlus Sunnat Wal Jamaat.

A.H.ELIAS(MUFTI)
1421/2001

ADMONITION FOR THE NEGLECTFUL

OSTENTATION IS A MINOR FORM OF POLYTHEISM.

Rasulullaah (sallAllaahu-alaihi-wasallam) has mentioned, "I greatly fear minor polytheism for you." When the Sahabahh (R.A) asked what 'minor polytheism' was, Rasulullaah (sailAllaahu-alaihi-wasallam) replied, "Ostentation."

On the Day of Judgement, those who were ostentatious will be told, "Go to those for whom you had carried out your actions in the world. Collect the rewards for your actions from them if they are able to give you anything!"

THE SIMILITUDE OF OSTENTATION.

A wise man once coined the similitude of a person who performs actions to show others as that person who fills his purse with stones instead of money. These will not help him at all. It will only make the purse seem heavy to others, who will think that he is wealthy. In a similar manner, the ostentatious person will appear to be pious to others, but he will receive no reward for his actions from Allaah.

SEVEN THINGS ARE WORTHLESS WITHOUT SEVEN THINGS.

A saint once said that a person's actions are worthless if he does seven things without doing another seven. These are:

1. He claims to fear Allaah, yet he does not abstain from sin. This claim is thus futile.

2. He aspires for reward from Allaah, yet he does not perform any good actions. (Although Allaah can reward a person without good actions, but Allaah requires that he does good).
3. He desires to do good actions, but he does not resolve to do so.

4. He prays for something, yet does not make an effort to acquire it. Only those who make an attempt will receive the guidance to attain their objective. Allaah says, **"We will certainly show the ways to those who strive for Us."**
5. He seeks forgiveness (with the tongue) without being remorseful (within the heart).
6. Without internal reformation, superficial actions are worthless.
7. Actions are wasted without sincerity (irrespective of the quantity).

A DOUBLE REWARD FOR AN ACTION COMING TO THE FORE.

A Sahabi (R.A) once asked Rasulullaah (sallAllaahu-alaihi-wasallam) whether he would be rewarded for an action that he performed secretly, but people had learnt about it and he felt pleased about this. Rasulullaah (sallAllaahu-alaihi-wasallam) replied that he would receive double the reward therefore, one reward for performing the actions secretly and the other for it becoming apparent.

Explanation: Performing a actions secretly denotes sincerity, for which a person will be rewarded. When the actions becomes apparent, others are encouraged to emulate the same. The person is then rewarded for encouraging others.

Rasulullaah (sallAllaahu-alaihi-wasallam) has said, "Whoever initiated a good practice in Islaam, will receive the reward of whoever practises the same thereafter." [Muslim]

However, it will be contrary to the requirement of sincerity that a person carries out an act secretly, but desires that it becomes known.

WHO ARE THE SINCERE ONES?

A person once asked a saint, "Who is a sincere person.?" He replied, "The sincere person is the one who conceals his good actions just as he conceals his evil actions." When it was asked what the pinnacle of sincerity was, he replied, "When you detest to be praised by people."

RECOGNIZING THE CHOSEN SERVANTS OF ALLAAH : - FOUR TRAITS.

Hadhrat Zun Noon Misri (A.R) was once asked how to recognize Allaah's chosen and special servants. He replied by saying that there were four traits by which they could be recognized. These are:

1. He forsakes ease and comfort.
2. He spends from the little that is in his possession.
3. He is content with his lowly status.
4. Praise and insult are the same to him.

FOUR SIGNS OF OSTENTATION.

1. Being negligent of good actions when in seclusion.
2. Performing good actions with eagerness when in the public's eye.
3. Excelling in the performance of those actions that attract praise.
4. Reducing the performance of those actions that people frown at. [From the lips of Hadhrat Ali (R. A)]

THE FORT FOR ACTIONS.

There are three things that serve a fort for actions. They are:

1. The realization that the inspiration to do a good action is from Allaah (this prevents pride and boastfulness).
2. To do every action for Allaah's pleasure.
3. To seek recompense for every action from Allaah only.

LEARN SINCERITY FROM A SHEPHERD.

A saint once advised that sincerity should be learnt from a shepherd. When someone asked how this was possible, he replied, "When the shepherd performs his salaah while tending to his goats, the thought never crosses his mind that the goats will praise him. In this manner, a person should carry out his acts of worship, being undeterred by the praises and insults of people."

FOUR CONDITIONS FOR THE ACCEPTANCE OF ACTIONS.

1. Knowledge. (Only that action performed with proper knowledge thereof will be accepted).
2. Intention. (Rasulullaah (sallAllaahu-alaihi-wasallam) said that the basis of all actions are their intentions).
3. Patience. (Actions should be performed calmly and all adversities encountered while performing a action should be borne patiently).
4. Sincerity.

HOW TO RECOGNIZE PIETY :- THREE FACTORS.

Someone once told Hadhrat Shafeeq bin Ibraheem (R.A), "People call me a pious person. How can piety be recognized?" The reply was, "It can be recognized by three factors. These are:

1. Explain your inner condition to the pious people. If they are satisfied, then you are pious, otherwise not.

2. Offer the world to your heart. If it refuses the world then you are pious, otherwise not.
3. Offer death to yourself. If you are pleased with it, then you are pious, otherwise not.

If a person has these three qualities, he should thank Allaah and display humility. He should then never allow ostentation to infect his actions, for this will pour water over all that he does."

THREE IMPORTANT FACTORS.

Certain saints always included the following three factors when writing a letter.

1. Allaah will amend the worldly matters of the person who works for the Hereafter.
2. Allaah will amend the relationship between people and the person who cares to rectify his relationship with Allaah (i.e. he is sincere to Allaah).

3. Allaah will correct the external aspects of the person who corrects his internal self. [From Hadhrat Auf bin Abdullaah (R.A)]

THREE FACTORS CAUSE DESTRUCTION.

Allaah causes a person to be involved in three things when He intends to destroy him. These are:

1. Allaah grants him knowledge without the inspiration to practise thereupon.
2. Allaah allows him the company of the righteous, without the recognition of their status and appreciation of them.
3. Allaah allows him to do good actions without sincerity.

These are all a result of incorrect intentions. If a person acts with the correct intention, he will be practical on his knowledge, will appreciate the company of the righteous and will perform all actions with sincerity.

THE FOUR NAMES OF A BOASTFUL PERSON.

Someone asked Rasulullaah (sallAllaahu-alaihi-wasallam) about which acts will secure salvation in the Hereafter. The reply was, "Do not deceive Allaah." When the meaning of this was asked, Rasulullaah (sallAllaahu-alaihi-wasallam) said, "Act on Allaah's orders solely for Him, not for anyone besides Him. Performing a action for anyone besides Allaah will be deceiving Him. Guard against ostentation because this is shirk. The ostentatious person will be called by four names on the Day of Judgement (viz.) 'Oh Kaafir!' 'Oh Faajir!' (Oh sinner!), 'Oh Ghaadir!' (Oh deceiver!) and 'Oh Khaasir!' (Oh loser!) (Then they will be told,) 'Your actions are wasted and your rewards spent.There is no share for you here and the deceiver should collect his reward from the one for whom he acted."

The Sahabi (R.A) who narrated this hadith swore by Allaah that he heard this hadith from Rasulullaah (sallAllaahu-alaihi-wasallam).

Someone has said the following fine words, "Safeguarding a action is more difficult than performing it."

THE SIMILITUDE OF GOOD ACTIONS.

Hadhrat Abu Bakr Waasiti (R.A) has mentioned that a good action is like fine glass. Just a little heedlessness will cause it to shatter, whereafter it will be irreparable. In the same way, good actions are shattered by ostentation and boastfulness, thus it will not accrue any reward.

Note: When a person senses any show and ostentation in a action, he should try his level best to eradicate it. If it cannot be eradicated, he should not abandon the action, but seek forgiveness from Allaah. Allaah may grant him the ability to be sincere in the following action.

AN INCIDENT.

A person doubted his sincerity after constructing an inn for travellers. Someone told him in a dream that even if his action was insincere, the du'as of the travellers who will benefit from this noble action will surely be sincere and accepted in your favour. He became extremely pleased and satisfied with this statement.

THE PANGS OF DEATH ARE A WORD OF CAUTION.

Hadhrat Hasan (R.A) narrates that Rasulullaah (sallAllaahu-alaihi-wasallam) said, "The pangs of death are equivalent to being struck by three hundred swords." He also mentioned that the pangs of death serve as an advice to my ummah.

APPRECIATING FIVE THINGS BEFORE FIVE.

Hadhrat Maymoon bin Mahraan (R.A) reports from Rasulullaah (sallAllaahu-alaihi-wasallam) that five things should be appreciated before five things. (1) Youth before old age. (2) Health before illness. (3) Leisure time before becoming busy. (4) Wealth before poverty. (5) Life before death.

୪ When old age arrives, it is difficult to even imagine performing those acts of worship performed in one's youth. In old age it is also extremely difficult to alter those bad habits and lethargy that one may have adopted during one's youth.

୪ The value of good health is only truly understood when one becomes ill. Therefore, it will definitely be tragic to waste one's time when enjoying good health.

୪ The nights are hours of leisure. If these are notutilized for dhikr and ibaadah, one will notpossibly be able to compensate for them duringthe busy hours of the day. This applies especiallyto the long winter nights. Also, when one lives affluently, he has more time at leisure and may misuse it in futility. Therefore, it is better to use ones time well so that one is not forced to change,laziness is cause of adversity.

WINTER IS A BLESSING FOR THE MU'MIN.

Rasulullaah (sallAllaahu-alaihi-wasallam) has said, "Winter is a blessing for the Mu'min. The nights are long, thereby enabling longer hours of worship. The days are short, thereby resulting in shorter fasts."

He has also said, "The night is long, so do not shorten it with sleep. The day is bright, so do not darken it with your sins."

A person should be content and happy with whatever Allaah gives. If a person attains contentment and satisfaction, then he should consider these as blessings and be thankful to Allaah. He should not aspire for the wealth that has been given to others.

All actions can be performed before death, therefore life should be regarded as a blessing and exploited to the full. Someone has mentioned golden words in Persian when he said, "If childhood is spent in play, old age in laziness, and youth in mischief, when will one worship Allaah?"

THE GRAVE IS EITHER A GARDEN OF JANNAH OR A PIT OF JAHANNAM.

Rasulullaah (sallAllaahu-alaihi-wasallam) has mentioned that the grave can either be a garden of Jannah (for the true Mu'min) or a pit of Jahannam (for the sinner and kaafir). Therefore, remember death often, which will destroy the carnal passions."

THE SIMILITUDE OF DEATH.

Hadhrat Umar (R.A) once asked Hadhrat Ka'b (R.A) to describe death. He said, "The similitude of death is like a thorny tree that is entered into the stomach of a person. The thorns then penetrate each and every vein and sinew of his. Then a strong person pulls the tree out with such force that it emerges, ripping the flesh as it is drawn out. This is the example of the throngs of death."

THREE THINGS SHOULD NOT BE FORGOTTEN.

A saint once said that an intelligent person must never forget three things. These are:-
(1) The perishable nature of this world,
(2) death and
(3) those adversities from which man cannot be secure.

ONLY FOUR PERSONS APPRECIATE FOUR THINGS.

1. Only an old man appreciates the value of youth.
2. Only a person afflicted with a calamity can truly appreciate being free of troubles.
3. Only the sick appreciate health.
4. Only the dead appreciate life.

THE REALITY OF DEATH.

Hadhrat Abdullaah bin Amr bin Al Aas (R.A) says that his father [Hadhrat Amr bin Al Aas (R.A)] used to often say, "I am surprised at the person upon whom the signs of death have appeared, yet he does not describe the reality thereof, even though his senses are still with him and his tongue can still talk."

When death began to approach him and he was still conscious and able to speak, the son asked, "Oh Father! You used to express surprise at those who do not describe the reality of death. Tell us about death." He replied, "Oh my son! It is not possible to describe the condition of death, but I will try. By Allaah! It seems as if a mountain has been placed between my shoulders, as if my soul is emerging from the eye of a needle and as if my stomach is filled with thorns. Oh my son! It seems as if the earth and the skies have joined and I am being crushed between the two."

WHEN ACTIONS CONTRADICT WORDS :- 4 THINGS

Hadhrat Shaqeeq bin Ibraheem (R.A) said, "People say four things with their tongues, but their actions contradict them.

(1) Every person claims that he is Allaah's slave, yet they act as if they are the slaves of none and that 'none' is their master.

(2) People say that Allaah is the Sustainer, yet their hearts are not content without the wealth of the world.

(3) People claim that the Aakhirat (Hereafter) is better than this world, yet they spend day and night accumulating the things of this world and do not even distinguish between halaal and haraam.

(4) They claim that death is certain, yet they act like people who will never die."

THREE THINGS ARE ASTONISHING.

Hadhrat Abu Dharr (R.A) said "There are three things that astonish me so much that they make me laugh, while another three things are so distressing that they make me cry. The three things that cause me to laugh in surprise are:

1. The person who aspires after the world when death is on his heels.
2. The negligent person, when Qiyamah is before him. (He believes in Qiyamah, yet does not prepare for death).
3. The person who laughs audaciously, yet he does not know whether Allaah is pleased with him or not.

The three things that are so distressing are:

1. Separation from my friends viz. Rasulullaah. (sallAllaahu-alaihi-wasallam) and the Sahabahh (R.A).
2. Death. (I do not know whether I will die with Imaan or not).

3.Standing before Allaah for reckoning, when I have no idea whether I will be sent to Jannah or to Jahannam.

DEATH DOES NOT ALLOW FATNESS.

Rasulullaah (sallAllaahu-alaihi-wasallam) has mentioned, "If the animals knew what you know of death, you will never be blessed with the opportunity of eating hearty flesh."

THE CONSEQUENCE OF REMEMBERING DEATH AND OF NOT REMEMBERING DEATH :- 3 BOUNTIES / 3 PUNISHMENTS.

Hadhrat Haamid (R.A) says that the person who abundantly remembers death will be honoured with three bounties.
(1) He will quickly receive the inspiration to repent.
(2) He will be content with whatever he receives.
(3) He will be resolute in his worship.

On the other hand, the person who does forget death will suffer three punishments.
(1) He will not be inspired to repent quickly.
(2) He will not be content with what he has.
(3) He will be lazy to worship.

THE TASTE OF DEATH IS EXTREMELY BITTER.

Someone once asked Hadhrat Isa (A.S) to raise a dead person for him. In compliance to the request, Allaah allowed him to raise the son of Hadhrat Nooh (A.S) by the name of Saam. When he got up from his grave, his hair and beard were white. Hadhrat Isa (A.S) enquired from him as to how his hair turned white, because there was no old age in their time.

He replied, "When I heard the call, I thought that Qiyamah had arrived. This fear caused me to turn white." When he was asked as to when he had died, he replied, "Four thousand years ago, but the taste of death has still not left me."

FOUR IMPORTANT FACTORS.

A person once told Hadhrat Ibraheem bin Adham (R.A) that they would be benefitted by the talks of Deen if he were to have a gathering with them. He said that four worries plagued his mind and he would only be able to sit with them if he could free himself from these. When he was asked what these four things were, he mentioned the following:

1. "My first concern is what Allaah said on the day that He took the pledge from people. Allaah said that certain people were destined for Jannah, while others were destined for Jahannam. I do not know which of the two groups I belong to.
2. When a child is in the womb of the mother, an angel asks Allaah whether he should record the child as fortunate or as an unfortunate one. I do not know how was I recorded.
3. When the angel of death claims a soul, he asks Allaah whether the soul should be kept with the Mu'mineen or with the kuffar. I do not know what reply will issue forth with regard to myself.
4. Allaah will announce on the Day of Judgement, **"Be separated, Oh you criminals."** I do not know to which party I will belong."

THE FOUR SIGNS OF A PERSON WHO AWAKENS FROM HIS NEGLIGENCE.

There are four signs that disclose the person who has shattered the inhibiting veils of negligence. These are:

1. He becomes one who is content and delays in the matters of the world.
2. He becomes a person who is anxious of the Hereafter and hastens in matters pertaining thereto.
3. He applies his thoughts for the Deen with knowledge and effort.
4. He is caring and cordial towards the creation.

THE BEST PERSON :- 5 TRAITS.

It has been said that the best person is he who possesses five traits.

1. He worships Allaah.
2. He is of use to the creation.
3. People are safe from his evils.
4. He is not aspirant of peoples' wealth.
5. He is always prepared for death.

THREE NOBLE QUALITIES.

Hadhrat Abu Darda (R.A) has mentioned that he loves the following three things:-

1. Destitution - so that he could be humble.
2. Illness- so that his sins would be forgiven.
3. Death- so that he could meet Allaah.

THE BEST AND MOST INTELLIGENT PERSON.

When someone asked Rasulullaah (sallAllaahu-alaihi-wasallam) who the best person was, he replied, "The one who has the best character." When it was asked as to who the most intelligent person was, the reply was, "The person who remembers death the most and prepares for it."

FIVE TYPES OF GLAD TIDINGS.

Allaah says, "**As for those who say, 'Our Rabb is Allaah!' then they are steadfast, We shall send angels to them saying, 'Do not fear and do not grieve. Accept the glad tidings of the Jannah that you have been promised.**" [Surah Mu'min]

THESE GLAD TIDINGS ARE OF FIVE TYPES, VIZ.

1. For the average Mu'min, it will mean that they will not fear suffering eternal punishment. Although they may have to suffer for a while, they will be removed and the Ambiyaa (A.S) will intercede on their behalf.
2. For the sincere ones, it will mean that they will not have to fear that their actions will be rejected. They will not have to grieve over the loss of rewards, for these will be granted double-fold to them.
3. For those who repented, it will mean that they do not have to fear for their sins. These will be forgiven and they will not have to fear whether their sins will be forgiven after Taubah.
4. For the asceticism, it will mean that they will not have to fear accountability and will receive the glad tidings of entering Jannah without reckoning.
5. For the religious scholars who propagated good and practiced on their knowledge, it will mean that they will not have to fear the torment and terror of Qiyamah. They will not have to grieve over the loss of rewards. They and their followers will be given the tidings of entering Jannah.

The grave of the Mu'min. The grave of a Mu'min will be expanded by seventy spans and a bedding of velvet will be laid for him therein. The grave will be fragrant and illuminated with the light of Imaan and the Qur'aan. He will then be made to sleep like a bride, to be awoken by her beloved.

The grave of a kaafir. The grave of the kaafir will be so much narrowed that his ribs will penetrate each other. A snake, the thickness of a camel's neck will continue to eat at his flesh and a deaf and dumb angel will continue to beat him with a hammer. The Fire of Jahannam will be shown to him each day and night.

EIGHT THINGS THAT WILL SAVE ONE FROM THE PUNISHMENT OF THE GRAVE.

Faqih Abul Laith Samarqandi (R.A) mentioned that carrying out four things and abstaining from another four things will protect one from punishment in the grave. The four things to practice on are:-
(1) Punctuality with salaah,
(2) abundant charity,
(3) recitation of the Qur'aan,
(4) abundance of dhikr.

The four that have to be avoided are:
(1) Lying,
(2) misappropriation of trust,
(3) carrying tales,
(4) droppings of urine (from contaminating the body and clothes).

Rasulullaah (sallAllaahu-alaihi-wasallam) has mentioned that punishment in the grave is usually due to droppings of urine.

ALLAAH DETESTS FOUR THINGS IN PARTICULAR.

1. Playing in salaah.
2. Futile speech while the Qur'aan is being recited.
3. Cohabitation while fasting.
4. Laughing in the graveyard.

A GOLDEN SAYING.

Standing by the side of a graveyard, the great illuminary, Hadhrat Muhammad bin Sammaak (R.A) said, "The silence and equality of the graves should not deceive you. There are many distressed and alarmed people therein, and there is a great difference between all these graves. The intelligent person is he who prepared for the grave before entering it."

A STARTLING INCIDENT.

Some people told Hadhrat Abdullaah bin Abbaas (R.A) that they dug a grave to bury a companion of theirs. They found a black snake therein. When they dug the second and third graves, they saw the same snake therein. They asked him what they were to do.

He advised them to bury him in any of these graves. He told them that the snake was a consequence of one of his actions and that they would find it present even if they dug every grave in the world. After burying him, they met his wife, who told them that he used to sell grains and that daily he would take out some for eating, replacing these with stones or sticks.

THE ANNOUNCEMENTS OF THE EARTH:- 5 CALLS.

Daily the earth makes five announcements:

1. Oh Man! You walk on my back and will be within my belly one day.
2. Oh Man! You eat various things on my back and will be eaten by worms and insects in by belly.
3. Oh Man! You laugh while on my back. Soon you will be crying within my belly.
4. Oh Man! You are happy on my back. Soon you will be grieved when you enter my belly.
5. Oh Man! You perpetrate sins on my back and soon will be punished in my belly.

AN ALARMING INCIDENT.

Hadhrat Amr bin Dinaar (R.A) reports that a man who lived in Madinah had a sister in the same district. He buried her after her death, but realized afterwards that he had dropped his wallet in the grave. He took someone with him to the graveyard and they found the grave which they dug.

After finding the wallet, he told the person to dig deeper so that they could see the condition of his sister. As he peeped therein he saw flames leaping from within. Startled, he had the grave filled and went to see his mother. At first his mother refused to disclose the condition of her daughter, but when the man insisted, she told him that his sister used to delay in the performance of her salaah and perform it after it's time. She also said that the girl never performed her wudhu properly and would eavesdrop on people at night so as to relate their conversations to others.

THE SCREAMS OF THE DEAD.

Rasulullaah (sallAllaahu-alaihi-wasallam) mentioned that everything besides man can hear the screams of the dead. If man heard it, he would fall unconscious. The pious deceased tells the people to hasten with his bier for, if they saw where he was heading, they would hurry thereto themselves. The evil soul pleads with the people not to hurry for, if they saw where he was going, they would never take him there.
After burial, two dark , blue-eyed angels appear before the deceased. Salaah prevents them from approaching near the head side saying, "Do not approach from this direction because he used to engage in salaah during the night for fear of the grave. Obedience to parents will shield him from the side of his feet, charity from the right side, and fasting from the left.

This world is but for a few days, whereafter the everlasting journey to the Hereafter commences. There a person will not be able to recite SubhaanAllaah' or Alhamdulillah' even once. The life in this world is the only capital that a person has to invest for the Hereafter. If the capital is exhausted, a person cannot do any business. Time passes by constantly. When he decides to act it might be too late. **The angel Hadhrat Israfeel (A.S) is presently waiting with the trumpet in his mouth- waiting for Allaah's command to blow it. Once he blows the trumpet, all of creation will be overcome with a strange anxiety. When he blows it for the second time, the universe will be annihilated, except for a few angels. Thereafter Allaah will ask the angel of death, "Who is still alive?" He will submit, "Jibraeel, Mika'eel, Israfeel, the angels who carry the Arsh and myself."**

Allaah will then command him to extract the souls of all these angels. When he will do so, Allaah will again ask him who else still lives. He will reply, "Besides Yourself, it is only me." Allaah will tell him, "All must perish besides Myself so you also die." Consequently, the angel of death will extract his own soul between Jannah and Jahannam. He shall give such an agonizing cry at that time that if any of the creation existed then, they would all die on account of this cry.

He will then say, "If I realized the pain of death I would have been even more gentle when extracting the souls of the Mu'mineen."

Only Allaah shall live on. He will announce, "Where are the kings? Where are the princes? Where have the tyrants gone? Where are their children? Where are those who ate from My provisions? **To whom does sovereignty belong today? It all belongs to Allaah, The One, The Mighty."**
Thereafter Allaah will cause a resuscitating rain to fall from the skies, causing people to surface from their graves like sprouting plants. Thereafter Hadhrat Israfeel (A.S) will be raised, followed by Hadhrat Jibreel and Mikaa'eel (A.S). Then Hadhrat Israfeel (A.S) will blow the trumpet for the third time and all of creation will be brought back to life. The first to be raised will be Rasulullaah (sallAllaahu-alaihi-wasallam). Everyone will be naked and will be gathered on a grand plain. Allaah will not turn His attention to the people to pass judgement, and they will weep so much that their tears will deplete and be replaced by blood. People will

perspire so much that the perspiration of some of them will reach till their mouths.

The people will then go to all the Ambiyaa (A.S), pleading with them to beseech Allaah to commence the reckoning. However, all will refuse except Rasulullaah (sallAllaahu-alaihi-wasallam). After his intercession on their behalf, Allaah will begin the reckoning. All the angels will stand in rows and it will be announced, "Everyone's actions have been recorded in their books. Those whose actions were good should thank Allaah and those whose actions were evil have only themselves to blame. All creation besides man and jinn will have their revenge from each other, whereafter they will perish forever."

No monetary recompense will work there. A wrongdoer will have to repay the claimant with his good actions. When their good actions have expired, they will be laden with the evil actions of the people who claim from them. In this manner many people who initially had many good actions will end up bankrupt. The oppressor will then be doomed for Jahannam, while the oppressed person will enter Jannah.

The day will be so severe that even the Ambiyaa (A.S), the high ranking angels and the martyrs will doubt their predicament. Questions will be asked about one's life, youth, knowledge and wealth. In search of a single action, people will approach their children, parents and loved ones, but will return empty handed.

Hadhrat Anas (R.A) reports that once Hadhrat Jibreel (A.S) came to Rasulullaah (sallAllaahu-alaihi-wasallam) in such a state that he was overcome with fear and his face had become pale. Rasulullaah (sallAllaahu-alaihi-wasallam) had never seen him in this condition before. When Rasulullaah (sallAllaahu-alaihi-wasallam) enquired about the reason for this condition, Hadhrat Jibreel (A.S) replied that he had seen such a scene from Jahannam. On such a day when no person (who had seen the same) would rest until he was assured protection therefrom.

Rasulullaah (sallAllaahu-alaihi-wasallam) then asked him to describe what he saw. He said, "When Allaah created Jahannam, he stoked the fire for a thousand years until it was red. Thereafter He stoked it for another thousand years until it became white. He then kindled it for another thousand years until it became as black and dark as it is presently.

The flames and coals of Jahannam never remain silent. By Allaah! If even the extent of a needle's eye of Jahannam was released to this world, the entire universe would burn to cinders."

"If the clothing of a person from Jahannam was to be suspended between the earth and the sky, the stench and heat emitting therefrom would kill the entire universe. If a single chain from the 'Salaasil' mentioned in the Qur'aan is placed upon a mountain, it would melt and sink below the surface. If a person in the east was afflicted with the punishment of Jahannam, the people in the west would be scorched with the heat."

"The heat of Jahannam is extremely intense and it is exceptionally deep. The jewellery of the person in Jahannam will be iron, his drink will be boiling puss and his clothing will be fire. Jahannam has seven doors. Every man and woman entering each door has been specified."

Rasulullaah (sallAllaahu-alaihi-wasallam) asked him whether the doors were like those of earthly homes. He replied, "No. They are more vast on the top and beneath. Their width is a distance of seventy years and each door is seventy times hotter than the next. The enemies of Allaah will be dragged to the doors and will be received with yokes and chains. When a chain is put in their mouths it will emerge from their posteriors. Their hands will also be handcuffed."

"With each human in Jahannam there will be a shaytaan. The angels will then drag them on their faces into Jahannam, beating them with iron hammers. Whenever they will try to escape from Jahannam they will be beaten back."

Rasulullaah (sallAllaahu-alaihi-wasallam) enquired from Hadhrat Jibreel (A.S) as to who will be in all these various doors. Hadhrat Jibreel (A.S) replied, "The lowest door (level) will be for the munafiqeen, the people of the Maa'idah and the people of Fir'oun. This level is called 'Haawiya.' On the next level, called 'Jaheem,' will be the Mushrikeen, while the Sabaians will occupy the third level, which is called 'Saqar.' Iblees and his comrades will be in the fourth level called 'Lazaa,' and the fifth level, known as 'Hutama' is reserved for the Jews. The Christians will then be on the sixth level called 'Sa'eer."

Thereafter Hadhrat Jibreel (A.S) remained silent, whereupon Rasulullaah (sallAllaahu-alaihi-wasallam) asked, "Why have you remained silent? Who will occupy the seventh level?" Feeling ashamed, Hadhrat Jibreel (A.S) said, "This level will be occupied by those members of your ummah who commit major sins and die without repenting." Unable to bear this Rasulullaah (sallAllaahu-alaihi-wasallam) fell down unconscious. Hadhrat Jibreel (A.S) then took the head of Rasulullaah (sallAllaahu-alaihi-wasallam) upon his lap. When Rasulullaah (sallAllaahu-alaihi-wasallam) recovered he asked Hadhrat Jibreel (A.S) whether any members of his ummah will really enter Jahannam. Hadhrat Jibreel (A.S) replied, "Yes. Those who commit major sins and die without repenting." Rasulullaah (sallAllaahu-alaihi-wasallam) then burst out in tears and Hadhrat Jibreel (A.S) also did the same.

After this Rasulullaah (sallAllaahu-alaihi-wasallam) only left the house for salaah and did not mix with anyone. He would begin and terminate the salaah in tears. On the third day Hadhrat Abu Bakr (R.A) came to the house of Rasulullaah (sallAllaahu-alaihi-wasallam) and requested permission to enter. When he received no reply he returned in tears.

The same happened to Hadhrat Umar (R.A). Thereafter Hadhrat Salmaan Farsi (R.A) also requested permission to enter and he was extremely perturbed when he did not receive a reply. In his anxiety he stood awhile, then sat, then returned to his home, only to go back to the house of Rasulullaah (sallAllaahu-alaihi-wasallam). He then went to the house of Hadhrat Faatima (R.A). When he related the incident to her, she immediately adorned her shawl and proceeded to the house of her father (sallAllaahu-alaihi-wasallam).
Arriving at the door she greeted with salaam and said that she was Faatima. At that time Rasulullaah (sallAllaahu-alaihi-wasallam) was prostrating and weeping for his ummah. He then raised his head and exclaimed, "The coolness of my eyes Faatima! What is the matter?" He then asked his wife to allow Hadhrat Faatima (R.A) in. When she noticed how pale her father had become and that exuberance from his face was missing, she began to weep most bitterly. When she asked him the reason for this condition of his, Rasulullaah (sallAllaahu-alaihi-wasallam) replied, "Hadhrat Jibreel (A.S) has informed me about the conditions in Jahannam and told me that the uppermost level will be occupied by those people of my ummah who commit major

sins and die without repenting. This has caused me the grief that you see."

She enquired from Rasulullaah (sallAllaahu-alaihi-wasallam) about the condition in which these people will be entered into Jahannam. Rasulullaah (sallAllaahu-alaihi-wasallam) replied, "The angels will drag them into Jahannam, but their faces will not be darkened, their eyes will not be blue, their mouths will not be sealed, there will be no shaytaan with them and they will not be shackled in chains and yokes."

She then asked how will they be dragged into Jahannam. Rasulullaah (sallAllaahu-alaihi-wasallam) replied by saying that the men will be dragged by their beards and the women by their hair. These people, male and female, young and old, will scream and cry because of the disgrace that they suffer. When they will be brought to Jahannam, the doorkeeper (Maalik) will enquire, "Who are these people? They are unique because their faces are not darkened, their eyes are not blue, their mouths are not sealed, there are no shayateen with them, and they are not shackled in yokes and chains."

The angels will reply that they have no knowledge about the identities of these people and that they were merely commanded to present them to him. He will then address them saying, 'Oh you wretched ones! You tell me who you are." [According to another narration, they will shout, "Oh Muhammad (sallAllaahu-alaihi-wasallam)! Oh Muhammad (sallAllaahu-alaihi-wasallam)!" as they will be dragged. However, they will forget this when they see the doorkeeper of Jahannam].

When he asks them, they will reply, 'We are those to whom the Qur'aan was revealed and upon whom the fasts on Ramadhaan were made compulsory.' He will say, 'But the Qur'aan was revealed to Muhammad (sallAllaahu-alaihi-wasallam).' Upon hearing this they will exclaim, 'We are from the ummah of Rasulullaah (sallAllaahu-alaihi-wasallam).' Maalik will tell them, 'Did the Qur'aan not warn you against disobeying Allaah?"

When they see the fire from the door, they will plead with him to allow them to weep over themselves. They will the weep till their tears dry up and is replaced by tears of blood. As they weep, he will tell them, 'If only this weeping had taken place in the world, then you would not have been weeping here.' They will then be cast into Jahannam by his command.

As they are thrown therein, they will all cry out in one voice saying, "Laa ilaaha IllAllaah." Upon hearing this, the fire will withdraw from them. When Maalik will enquire about this, the fire will submit, 'How could I seize them when their tongues hymn the kalimah of Tauheed?" When this will recur several times Maalik will say that they can only be burned when Allaah commands.

The fire will reach till the feet of some of them, till the knees of others, till the waists of others and up to the throats of some. When the fire will approach their faces, Maalik will instruct the fire not to burn their faces and their hearts because they prostrated in salaah and observed fasts during Ramadhaan. These people will suffer for their sins and remain in Jahannam till Allaah desires that they should emerge therefrom. They will constantly call out, 'Ya Hannaan! Ya Mannaan! Ya Arhamar Raahimeen!"

Eventually a day will come when Allaah will instruct Hadhrat Jibreel (A.S) to find out about the ummah of Rasulullaah (sallAllaahu-alaihi-wasallam). He will hasten to Jahannam and will find Maalik on a pulpit in the centre of Jahannam. Maalik will rise to receive him and will enquire about the reason for his visit. Hadhrat Jibreel (A.S) will reply that he had arrived to find out about the ummah of Rasulullaah (sallAllaahu-alaihi-wasallam).

Maalik will reply that they are in a miserable condition and in a very confined place. He will add that the fire had burnt all of their bodies except their faces and hearts. These two will still glow with the light of Imaan. Hadhrat Jibreel (A.S) will request to see them. When they see Hadhrat Jibreel (A.S), they will realize that he is not one of the angels of punishment. They will not have seen such a beautiful countenance before. They will be told that this is Hadhrat Jibreel (A.S), who brought revelation to Hadhrat Muhammad (sallAllaahu-alaihi-wasallam). Upon hearing his name, they will call out, 'Oh Jibreel! Convey our salaams to our leader Rasulullaah (sallAllaahu-alaihi-wasallam) and tell him that our sins have separated us from him and destroyed us.' When Hadhrat Jibreel (A.S) will return to Allaah and relate the incident to Him, Allaah will ask him what these people requested him to do. He will say that they requested that their salaams be conveyed to Rasulullaah (sallAllaahu-alaihi-wasallam) and that he be informed of their condition. Allaah will command him to fulfill the request.

He will hasten to Rasulullaah (sallAllaahu-alaihi-wasallam), who will be relaxing in a palace made of pearl. It shall have four thousand entrances, each one having two doors of gold. After greeting with salaam, Hadhrat Jibreel (A.S) will tell Rasulullaah (sallAllaahu-alaihi-wasallam) that he had just returned from the sinners of his ummah. He will tell Rasulullaah (sallAllaahu-alaihi-wasallam) that these people had conveyed their salaams to him and wished to inform him of their miserable plight.

Hearing this, Rasulullaah (sallAllaahu-alaihi-wasallam) will immediately fall in prostration beneath Allaah's throne and praise Allaah with such words that he never knew before. Allaah will say, "Oh Muhammad! Raise your head. Ask and you will be granted. If you wish to intercede then do so. Your intercession will surely be accepted."

Rasulullaah (sallAllaahu-alaihi-wasallam) will submit, "Oh my Rabb! Your decision has been passed with regard to the sinful ones of my ummah and they have been punished for their sins. Please accept my intercession on their behalf." Allaah will declare, "The command has been issued and your intercession is accepted. You go personally and remove from Jahannam every person who recited "Laa ilaaha IllAllaah." Rasulullaah (sallAllaahu-alaihi-wasallam) will then approach the doorkeeper of Jahannam. Upon seeing him, Maalik will rise in reverence. Rasulullaah (sallAllaahu-alaihi-wasallam) will say, "Oh Maalik! How are the sinners of my ummah?" Maalik will reply by saying that their condition is miserable inaction. When the door of Jahannam will be opened, the sinful Muslims in Jahannam will cry out, "Oh Rasulullaah (sallAllaahu-alaihi-wasallam)! The fire has burnt our skins and livers."

Rasulullaah (sallAllaahu-alaihi-wasallam) will remove them all from Jahannam and they will appear as black as charcoals. He will then bath them in the river of Ridhwaan, which is one of the rivers at the entrance of Jannah. After being bathed, they will emerge as resplendent youths with their faces shining like the full moon. On their foreheads will be emblazoned, "This is a person from Jahannam whom Allaah has emancipated."

They will then all be admitted into Jannah, whereupon the other inmates of Jahannam will wish that they had also been Muslims so that they could be removed from Jahannam. Allaah says in the Qur'aan, **"Many a time the disbelievers wish that they were Muslims."**

It will be then that death shall be presented as a sheep and slaughtered before the people of Jannah and the people of Jahannam. They will then be told, "Now none shall ever die. Each person will remain forever where he is." [May Allaah save us all from Jahannam. Aameen.]

The reality of Jannah: Hadhrat Abu Huraira (R.A) narrates that the Sahabahh (R.A) once asked Rasulullaah (sallAllaahu-alaihi-wasallam) what Jannah was made of. He replied, "From water." Thereupon they asked, "We wish to know about the buildings of Jannah." Rasulullaah (sallAllaahu-alaihi-wasallam) said, "One brick is of gold, another of silver, and the mortar is musk. The sand is Saffron and the pebbles are pearls and rubies. Whoever will enter Jannah will not be deprived of any bounty, and will abide therein forever. They will never die therein, their clothing will never wear out and their youth shall never terminate."

Thereafter Rasulullaah (sallAllaahu-alaihi-wasallam) continued to say, "The du'as of three people are never rejected. They are:
(1) A just ruler,
(2) the fasting person when he terminates his fast, and
(3) the oppressed person. Their du'as are lifted above the clouds and Allaah responds by saying, 'I shall definitely assist you even though it may be after some time."

THE TREES OF JANNAH.

Rasulullaah (sallAllaahu-alaihi-wasallam) said that a person of Jannah will walk beneath the shadow of a tree for a hundred years without emerging therefrom. He said that there are such bounties in Jannah which no eye has ever seen, no ear has ever heard of and no heart or mind has ever yearned. Thereafter Rasulullaah (sallAllaahu-alaihi-wasallam) recited the verse, **"A soul does not know what has been concealed there to cool his eyes."**

Rasulullaah (sallAllaahu-alaihi-wasallam) then added that a place in Jannah measuring the size of a whip is better than this world and everything contained therein.

ONE OF THE DAMSELS OF JANNAH CALLED LA'IBA.

Hadhrat Abdullaah bin Abbaas (R.A) reports that Rasulullaah (sallAllaahu-alaihi-wasallam) said, "There is a damsel in Jannah called La'iba. She was created from a mixture of musk, amber, camphor, saffron and the 'water of life.' All the other damsels of Jannah love her. If she has to spit in the ocean, the waters will become sweet. The following words appear on her forehead: "Whoever desires me should obey his Rabb."

Hadhrat Mujaahid (R.A) says that the ground of Jannah is silver, the sand is musk, the trunks of the trees are silver and the branches are of pearls and crystal. The fruit will be easy to reach whether a person is sitting, standing or lying down.

THE BEAUTY OF THE PEOPLE OF JANNAH.

Hadhrat Abu Huraira (R.A) reports that the beauty and youth of the people of Jannah will continue to increase just as old age gradually overtakes the people of this world.

THE GREATEST BOUNTY OF JANNAH.

Hadhrat Suhaib (R.A) narrates from Rasulullaah (sallAllaahu-alaihi-wasallam) that when the people of Jannah will enter Jannah and the inmates of Jahannam will enter Jahannam, a caller will announce, "Oh people of Jannah! Allaah wishes to fulfill the promise that he made to you." They will enquire, "What can this bounty be? Has Allaah not caused our scales to be weighty, our faces to be illuminated, admitted us into Jannah and saved us from Jahannam?"

The veils will then be lifted (from Allaah) and the people of Jannah will see Allaah. Rasulullaah (sallAllaahu-alaihi-wasallam) added, "By Allaah! There will be nothing more beloved and better for the people of Jannah." (May Allaah bless us all with this privilege. Aameen.)

HADHRAT JIBREEL (A.S) APPEARS IN A STRANGE MANNER TO CONVEY GLAD TIDINGS.

Hadhrat Anas (R.A) narrates that once Hadhrat Jibreel (A.S) came to Rasulullaah (sallAllaahu-alaihi-wasallam) with a bright mirror wherein there was a black spot. When Rasulullaah (sallAllaahu-alaihi-wasallam) asked him what the mirror was, he replied, "This is the day of Jumu'ah and the spot is that moment in every Jumu'ah (wherein du'as are accepted). You and your ummah have been favoured above the previous ummahs with this. There is a moment during this day wherein every du'a is accepted. This day is the day of 'Mazeed."

Rasulullaah (sallAllaahu-alaihi-wasallam) enquired, "What is the day of 'Mazeed?" Hadhrat Jibreel (A.S) replied, "Allaah has created a valley in Jannah wherein there is a container of musk. Every Jumu'ah, pulpits of celestial light are placed therein and the Ambiyaa (A.S) ascend them. There are also golden pulpits studded with rubies and crystal whereupon the Siddiqeen, martyrs and righteous people will sit. The people of Ghuraf (the average person of Jannah) will sit on hillocks nearby. They will all engage in praising Allaah."

Allaah will tell them, "Supplicate to Me and all your supplications will be accepted." They will all pray for Allaah's pleasure. Thereupon Allaah will say, "I am pleased with all of you. I granted you a place in My home and conferred honour upon you." Thereafter Allaah's brilliance will be made manifest to them and they all will witness it. Due to this extra bounty, they will not find any day more beloved to them than the day of Jumu'ah.

According to one narration, Allaah will tell the angels, "Feed My friends." They will then serve various types of foods, each morsel having a different taste. They will then be served various types of drinks by Allaah's command, each sip having a different taste.

Thereafter Allaah will tell them, "I am your Rabb and I have fulfilled that promise that I had made to you. I will now fulfill whatever requests you make." The people of Jannah will repeatedly say that they only desire Allaah's pleasure. Allaah will tell them, "I am pleased with you and I have something else with Me. Today I will bestow such a bounty on you that is superior to all of this."

Consequently, the veils will be removed and everyone will witness Allaah's magnificence. They will immediately fall into prostration and will remain in this position until Allaah tells them, "Raise your heads. This is not a place of worship." The people of Jannah will forget all the bounties of Jannah upon witnessing this sight. Then a strong wind will blow from beneath the Arsh. Musk will emanate from a white container and fall on their heads and on the foreheads of their horses. When they return to their abodes, their wives will say, "Today you have returned even more handsome than you were."

Hadhrat Ikrama (R.A) reports that the men and women of Jannah will all be youths of 33 years. They will all be extremely good looking and will each wear seventy sets of clothing. They will see their reflections on the faces, chests and calves of their spouses. A hadith mentions that if a damsel of Jannah has to expose her palm from the heavens, it would illuminate the entire universe.

THERE WILL BE NO NEED TO RELIEVE ONESELF IN JANNAH.

Hadhrat Zaid bin Arqam (R.A) says that a person from the Ahlul Kitaab asked Rasulullaah (sallAllaahu-alaihi-wasallam), "Will there be eating and drinking in Jannah?" Rasulullaah (sallAllaahu-alaihi-wasallam) replied, "Yes. A person will be given the strength of a hundred men, to eat, drink and cohabit."

The person commented that since a person needs to relieve himself after eating, how will he be able to do this in a pure place like Jannah? Rasulullaah (sallAllaahu-alaihi-wasallam) replied, "A person will not need to relieve himself in Jannah. However, his food will digest by means of perspiration which will have the fragrance of musk."

A TREE IN JANNAH CALLED "TOOBA."

A tree in Jannah called 'Tooba' will have a branch in every house of Jannah. It will bear various types of fruit, and birds, the size of camels, will perch thereupon. If a person of Jannah desires any of these birds, it will immediately be served on his table. He will be able to eat it dry on one side and roasted on the other. Thereafter the bird will get up and fly away.

THE APPEARANCE OF JANNAH.

Hadhrat Abdullaah bin Abbaas (R.A) and Hadhrat Abu Huraira (R.A) have reported from Rasulullaah (sallAllaahu-alaihi-wasallam), "The face of the first person to enter Jannah from my ummah will shine like the 14th full moon. The face of the second person will shine like a very bright star. Thereafter people will enter one after another with different appearances."

"There will be no need to relieve oneself in Jannah, neither will one's nose give out mucus. There will be combs of gold, rings of Ood(a fragrant perfume) and perspiration will have the fragrance of musk. Everyone's character will be alike. They will all be the youthful age of Hadhrat Isa (A.S) at 33. They will be as tall as Hadhrat Aadam (A.S) at 60 arm-lengths. They will be beardless and will have no hair besides that of their heads, eyebrows and eyelashes. They will be fair in complexion and their clothes will be green."

"When a person will lay his table, a bird will address him saying, 'Oh friend of Allaah! I have drank from the spring of Salsabeel and eaten a variety of fruit from the orchards beneath Allaah's Arsh.' The person of Jannah will eat from one side of the bird that will be cooked and from the other side, which will be roasted. He will also wear seventy sets of clothing, each set being different in colour."

He will wear ten rings. The following inscription will appear on the first ring: **"Peace be on you because of the patience that you have exercised."**

The second ring will have the inscription, **"Enter Jannah in peace and safety."**

The third will read: **"This is the Jannah that you have received in lieu of your good actions."**

The fourth will read: **"Grief and worry have been removed from you."**

The fifth will read: **"We have adorned you with jewels and beautiful garments."**

The sixth will read: **"We have wedded you to the Hoorul Ain."**

The seventh will read: **"You shall have in Jannah whatever your heart desires and whatever cools the eyes. And you shall abide therein forever."**

The eighth will read: **"You have conformed with the Ambiyaa (A.S) and the Siddiqeen."**

The ninth will read: **"You have become youths who will never age."**

The tenth will read: **"You are the neighbours of such people who never cause you difficulty."**

FIVE CONDITIONS FOR ADMISSION INTO JANNAH.

1. Abstention from all sins. Allaah says, **"He who restrains himself from passions, then Jannah will surely be his abode."**
2. Contentment with the basics of life.
3. Extreme eagerness to obey Allaah's commands because Jannah will be the reward for good actions. (Refer to the inscription on the third ring).
4. Having love for the pious servants of Allaah. Meeting them and participating in their gatherings because their intercession will be invaluable on the Day of Judgement. Rasulullaah (sallAllaahu-alaihi-wasallam) has mentioned, "Take the pious as brothers (friends) because every brother will be given the right to intercede on the Day of Judgement."

5. Supplicate in abundance, especially for Jannah and a pleasant death.

WORDS OF WISDOM :- 3 FACTS.

1. Look at the rewards to be attained in the Hereafter. It is foolish to be inclined towards the things of the world and rely on them despite possessing proper knowledge.
2. Helplessness is not to make an effort for actions despite possessing the knowledge of their rewards in the Hereafter.
3. That person will attain the comforts of Jannah who forsakes the comforts of this world. That person will be wealthy in Jannah who forsakes this perishable world and is content with just a little.

THE STORY OF AN ASCETIC.

An ascetic saint was eating some greens with only a bit of salt. When someone objected to this he replied, "I use the world for worship (i.e. so that I may derive strength for worship by eating, thereby attaining Jannah). On the other hand, you eat the delicacies of the world simply to convert them into excreta."

Note: It is not possible for every person to act as this ascetic did. It is advisable to utilize every bounty of Allaah and then show gratitude for the same. Allaah likes to witness the effects of His bounties on His servants. Allaah says, **"Display the bounties of your Rabb."**

A STORY OF HADHRAT IBRAHEEM BIN ADHAM (R.A).

Hadhrat Ibraheem bin Adham (R.A) once intended to use the public baths. The owner prevented him saying, "You cannot enter without first paying the fee." Hearing this Hadhrat Ibraheem (R.A) wept and said, "Oh Allaah! I am not allowed to enter the house of shaytaan without paying a fee.

Jannah is home of the Ambiyaa (A.S) and the Siddiqeen. How can I enter it without a fee (i.e. without good actions)?"

FOOD FOR THOUGHT.

Allaah once sent the following revelation to a Nabi (A.S): "Oh child of Aadam! You purchase Jahannam for an exorbitant price but fail to purchase Jannah for a small sum."

People consider spending exorbitant sums upon the prompting of some sinners, thereby purchasing Jahannam for themselves. However, they find it difficult to spend a small sum upon the request of a poor beggar, whereas this is the price for Jannah.

A STATEMENT OF HADHRAT ABU HAAZIM (R.A).

Hadhrat Abu Haazim (R.A) says, "If Jannah is attained by forsaking all the pleasures of the world, then this is a cheap bargain. Similarly, it will also be a cheap bargain if one attains salvation from Jahannam on account of enduring all types of difficulties. Jannah can also be attained by forsaking a single pleasure from a thousand pleasures and by enduring a single difficulty from a thousand difficulties. How cheap is this bargain?"

THE DOWRY FOR JANNAH.

Hadhrat Yahya bin Mu'aadh Raazi (R.A) says, "Forsaking this world may be difficult, but forsaking Jannah is much more difficult. The dowry for Jannah is the forsaking of this world."

THE INTERCESSION OF JANNAH AND JAHANNAM

Hadhrat Anas bin Maalik (R.A) says that if a person asks for Jannah thrice, then Jannah says to Allaah, "Oh Allaah! Admit him into Jannah." When a person seeks protection for Jahannam thrice, then Jahannam says to Allaah, "Oh Allaah! Protect him from Jahannam."

THE BAZAARS OF JANNAH.

Rasulullaah (sallAllaahu-alaihi-wasallam) has mentioned that there will be bazaars in Jannah, but there will be no trade therein. Friends will convene therein and speak about how they worshipped Allaah in the world, about the condition of the rich and the poor therein, about how death came to them and about the difficulties that they endured to reach Jannah.

WHO IS THERE WHO DESIRES JANNAH?

You have just read about the description of Jannah. Every person certainly desires to enter Jannah and must have made du'a for Jannah. However, to merely depend upon du'as without carrying out good actions is a deception. Foolish are those people who desire Jannah but are contaminated with sins and are negligent of performing good actions. They sleep when the mu'adhin calls the adhaan and sacrifice their salaah for their businesses. They are reluctant to pay zakaah and they forfeit their fasts in Ramadhaan. They die without performing the obligatory hajj and have no consideration for halaal and haraam in their businesses. They consider the learning and teaching of the Qur'aan as an iniquity and oppress the weak. They extract labour from the poor and usurp the wealth of orphans.

Despite carrying out all the above in addition to other sins, they aspire for high ranks of Jannah. If this is not foolishness, then what is? If one aspires for Jannah, he should devote his entire life to the commands of Allaah and the practices of Rasulullaah (sallAllaahu-alaihi-wasallam). At the same time, he should trample upon his carnal desires.

When the verse, "And My mercy encompasses everything," the accursed Iblees said that he is also part of "everything." Therefore he also began to aspire for Allaah's mercy. Similarly, the Jews and the Christians also began to think in this way. However, Iblees became despondent when the next part of the verse was revealed i.e. "I shall soon ordain this mercy for those who abstain from shirk, pay zakaah and who believe in Our verses."

However, the Jews and the Christians said, "We abstain from shirk, pay zakaah and believe in Allaah's verses." They also became despondent when the verse was revealed, "Those who follow the unlettered messenger."

Therefore, the verse only applied to the Mu'mineen. Every Mu'min should thank Allaah profusely for this great boon that Allaah has bestowed on him.

THE HOPE AND PRAYERS OF HADHRAT YAHYA BIN MU'AADH RAAZI (R.A):- 3 DUAAS.

Hadhrat Yahya bin Mu'aadh Raazi (R.A) used to make the following du'as:

1. Oh Allaah! You have sent one part of the hundred parts of Your mercy to this world, due to which we have been blessed with the priceless wealth of Islaam. So why should we not aspire for Your mercy on the day when You will exhibit the remainder of the hundred parts?

2. Oh Allaah! If Your reward is reserved for the obedient and Your mercy is for the sinners, I would aspire for Your reward even though I was not from the obedient. Therefore, why should I not aspire for Your mercy when I am a sinner?

3. Oh Allaah! You have created Jannah for Your friends and You have deprived the kuffar thereof and made them despondent of entering it. The angels are not in need of Jannah and You are also Independent of Jannah. Then for who can Jannah be besides for us?

NEVER MAKE ANYONE DESPONDENT OF ALLAAH'S MERCY.

Rasulullaah (sallAllaahu-alaihi-wasallam) once became displeased upon seeing some Sahabahh (R.A) laughing. He told them, "You people are laughing when Jahannam is behind you. I do not want to see you laughing again." Saying this, Rasulullaah (sallAllaahu-alaihi-wasallam) left.

We became so stiff that it seemed as if birds were perched on our heads. Rasulullaah (sallAllaahu-alaihi-wasallam) suddenly turned back and said, "Hadhrat Jibreel (A.S) has just come to me with a message from Allaah, 'You have made My bondsmen despondent of My mercy. Inform them that I am the Most Forgiving, the Most Merciful and that My punishment is most severe."

AN OATH MAY BE TAKEN ON FOUR THINGS.

Hadhrat Abdullaah bin Mas'ood (R.A) told Hadhrat Abdur Rahmaan (R.A), "I can take an oath on three things. If you take an oath on the fourth, I shall confirm your oath."

1. On the Day of Qiyamah, Allaah will only befriend those whom he befriended in the world.
2. Allaah shall never treat a Muslim (irrespective of the weakness of his Imaan) like how He will treat the kuffar.
3. A person will be with those whom he loves on the Day of Judgement.
4. On the Day of Qiyamah, Allaah will conceal the sins of those people whose sins He had concealed in the world.

INTERCESSION WILL BE ON BEHALF OF THE SINNERS.

Hadhrat Jaabir (R.A) narrates that Rasulullaah (sallAllaahu-alaihi-wasallam) said, "My intercession shall be for the sinful ones of my ummah. The one who rejects will be deprived of intercession."

A THOUGHT PROVOKING INCIDENT.

Hadhrat Jibreel (A.S) related to Rasulullaah (sallAllaahu-alaihi-wasallam) the incident of a person who lived on an island and worshipped Allaah for five hundred years. The island was surrounded by salty water, but Allaah caused a small spring of sweet water to flow near him, from which he drank. Allaah also caused a pomegranate tree to grow for him to eat from.

Daily he ate from the tree, drank from the water and made wudhu therewith. Allaah even accepted his du'a to die while prostrating. Hadhrat Jibreel (A.S) told Rasulullaah (sallAllaahu-alaihi-wasallam) that whenever they ascended and descended from the heavens they found him in prostration before Allaah.

On the Day of Judgement Allaah will announce that he should be admitted into Jannah on account of Allaah's mercy. He will submit that it will be on account of his worship. Allaah will then order that his actions be weighed against Allaah's bounties upon him. When this will be done, all five hundred years of worship will not even suffice for the power of sight that Allaah bestowed him with.

Allaah will then instruct the angels to take this person to Jahannam. As they proceed, he will say, "Oh Allaah! Enter me into Jannah by Your mercy." Allaah will then command the angels to bring him back. When they again present him before Allaah, Allaah will ask him the following questions:

Question: Who created you?

Reply: Oh Allaah! You did.

Question: Was this (creation) due to your actions or due to My mercy?

Reply: Due to Your mercy.

Question: Who granted you the guidance and the ability to engage in worship for five hundred years?

Reply: Oh Allaah! You did.

Question: Who took you to the island in the centre of the ocean? Who caused a spring of sweet water to flow amidst the salty water of the ocean? Who caused the pomegranate tree to grow? Who acceded to your request and allowed your soul to leave your body while you were prostrating?

Reply: Oh Allaah! You did.
Allaah will then tell him, "All of this was on account of My mercy, and I shall admit you into Jannah by My mercy as well."

GLAD TIDINGS.

The person whose heart contains fear and hope at the time of death will be treated according to his hope and saved from what he fears.

GOLDEN WORDS.

Hadhrat Ibn Mas'ood (R.A) narrates that Allaah's mercy will be so vast on the Day of Judgement that even shaytaan will anticipate mercy and intercession.

Hadhrat Fudail bin Ayaadh (R.A) says that fear is best while one is healthy, so that one may excel in good actions. However, during weakness and illness, hope is best so that one does not grow despondent.

A STUNNING INCIDENT ABOUT ALLAAH'S FORGIVENESS.

Hadhrat Ahmed bin Suhail (R.A) says that he saw Hadhrat Yahya bin Aktham (R.A) in a dream. He asked, "How did Allaah treat you?" He replied, "Allaah summoned me saying, 'Oh evil old man! You have perpetrated many bad acts.' I responded by saying, 'Oh my Rabb! I shall not comment on these at this moment.'

Allaah asked, 'Then what have you to say.' I said, 'Abdur Razzaaq told me that Zuhri told him that Urwa told him that Hadhrat A'isha (R.A) told him that Rasulullaah (sallAllaahu-alaihi-wasallam) told her that Hadhrat Jibreel (A.S) told him about Your declaration that 'When I wish to punish an old Muslim, I shy away due to his old age.' Oh Allaah! I am a very old man.

Allaah replied, 'They have all spoken the truth and so will it be.' I was therefore admitted to Jannah."

CONCISE ADVICE.

Hadhrat Umar (R.A) once came to Rasulullaah (sallAllaahu-alaihi-wasallam) and saw him weeping. When he enquired about the reason for the tears, Rasulullaah (sallAllaahu-alaihi-wasallam) said, "Allaah has declared that He feels ashamed to punish an old man because of his age, then why is the old man not ashamed to disobey Allaah?"

The tongue of every old person should be moist with excessive thanks to Allaah. He should be ashamed to sin before the scribe angels (Kiraamun Kaatibeen) and should therefore avoid all sins. He never knows when he will die. In fact, crops are harvested as soon as they ripen. Youth is expected after childhood, adulthood is expected after adolescence and old age is expected after adulthood. What can be expected after old age besides death?

SEVEN CATEGORIES OF PEOPLE WILL BE SHADED BENEATH THE THRONE OF ALLAAH.

Allaah's Arsh will shade seven categories of people on the Day of Qiyamah, when there shall not be any other shade. These shall be:

1. The just ruler.
2. The youth who engaged in Allaah's worship.
3. The person whose heart is attached to the masjid.
4. Those two persons who love each other solely for Allaah's pleasure.

5. The person who sheds tears when remembering Allaah in seclusion (this is a sign of sincerity).
6. The person who spends so secretly in charity that he does not even know how much he spends.
7. The person who, when he is seduced by a beautiful woman, withdraws saying, "I fear Allaah!"

A general and widespread punishment does not afflict the masses due to the sins of certain people. However, when sin becomes rampant and no one attempts to forbid it, then all and sundry are swept up in the wake of Allaah's punishment. [Hadhrat Umar bin Abdul Aziz (R.A)]

Faqih Abul Laith (R.A) says that Allaah once revealed to Rasulullaah Hadhrat Yusha bin Noon (A.S) that He would soon destroy 40 000 pious people of his nation and 60 000 of the sinful ones. He submitted, "The destruction of the sinful ones are understood, but why should the pious ones be destroyed?"

Allaah replied, "The pious ones did not forbid the evil and did not even consider the sins as an evil. In fact, they continued to eat, drink and mix with the sinners."

GLAD TIDINGS.

Rasulullaah (sallAllaahu-alaihi-wasallam) said, "Some people spread virtue and eradicate evil, while others spread evil and eradicate good. Glad tidings be for those whom Allaah has used to spread good and terminate evil. Destruction be to those who spread evil and terminate good."

RECOGNIZING A MU'MIN AND A HYPOCRITE.

Enjoining good and forbidding evil (Amr bil Ma'roof wan Nahy anil Munkar) is the hallmark of a Mu'min. Allaah says in the Qur'aan, **"The believing men and the believing women are auxiliaries to each other. They enjoin good and forbid evil."**

On the other hand, Allaah also says, **"The hypocrite men and women all proceed from one another. They enjoin evil and forbid from good."**

A REMARK BY HADHRAT ALI (R.A).

Hadhrat Ali (R.A) said, "The person who enjoins good, strengthens the firmness of the Mu'min, and the person who forbids evil, disgraces the hypocrite."

A TECHNIQUE IS REQUIRED WHEN ENJOINING GOOD.

Hadhrat Abu Darda (R.A) has mentioned that the person who advises his brother in public has humiliated him. The one who advises him in private has embellished him. (A person is more likely to accept advice given in private and will be encouraged by attempting to act thereupon).

TYRANNICAL RULERS ARE THE RESULT OF FAILURE TO ENJOIN GOOD AND FORBID EVIL.

Hadhrat Abu Darda (R.A) once said, "Oh people! Continue to practice Amr bil Ma'roof wan Nahy anil Munkar, otherwise Allaah will appoint such tyrants to rule over you, who will not respect your elders and will not have mercy upon your youngsters. Then the pious amongst you will pray to Allaah, but He will not accept their supplications. You will beseech His help, but He will not help you. You will seek His forgiveness, but He will not forgive you."

THE CATEGORIES OF ENJOINING GOOD AND FORBIDDING EVIL.

Rasulullaah (sallAllaahu-alaihi-wasallam) said, "When you see an evil being perpetrated, then prevent it with your hand. If you are unable to do this, then prevent it with your tongue. If you are unable to do even this, then at least consider it a vice in your heart. This is the lowest form of Imaan."

Some ulema have mentioned that rulers should forbid evil with their hands, the ulema should do so with their tongues, and the general public are those who at least consider it to be a vice.

A FASCINATING STORY.

A person was once infuriated when he noticed people worshipping a tree. He grabbed an axe and proceeded to chop it down. En route he met the accursed Iblees, who asked him where he was headed. He informed Iblees that he intended to chop the tree. Iblees bade him to leave the tree alone and let the worshippers suffer the consequences. An argument ensued and the two eventually wrestled thrice, Iblees being defeated each time.

When Iblees finally realized that he will never defeat the person, he adopted another approach. He told the person that if he left the tree to be, he would find four dirhams beneath his bed every morning. When the person hesitated, Iblees solemnly promised this for him. The person accepted the proposal and returned home. As promised, he found the four dirhams on the promised place each morning for several mornings. However, when he did not find anything for two consecutive mornings, he grabbed his axe in a fit of anger and again proceeded to the tree.

Again he met the accursed Iblees on the road. When Iblees asked him where he was going, he replied that he was on his way to cut down the tree that people were worshipping. Iblees then told him to back off because he would not allow him to proceed. Iblees said, "On the first occasion you wanted to cut the tree down for Allaah's pleasure and I would never been able to stop you despite my hardest efforts. Now you intend to chop it up on account of four dirhams. If you just take another step I will sever your head from your body!" The person was thus obliged to return home. This shows that when actions are done for Allaaah's pleaures, shaitaan is humbled. When actions are done for worldly benefit, even shaitaan gets bold.

FIVE CONDITIONS FOR A PREACHER.

1. Knowledge. (An ignorant person is not worthy of preaching).
2. Sincerity. (This is the lifeblood of every act and no action is accepted without it).
3. Good character and love. (The preaching of a harsh, impolite person cannot be effective).
4. Patience and forbearance. (A preacher cannot succeed without these two qualities because he will certainly encounter many difficulties and all types of people).

5. Practice upon what he preaches. (Without this his preaching will have no effect on the masses and he will fade away due to fear of peoples' taunts).

Hadhrat Hudhaifa (R.A) reports that Rasulullaah (sallAllaahu-alaihi-wasallam) said, "Oh people! You must practice Amr bil Ma'roof wan Nahy anil Munkar, otherwise Allaah's punishment may afflict you. Then you will supplicate to Him, but He will not accept your du'as." [Bukhari]

Rasulullaah (sallAllaahu-alaihi-wasallam) has also mentioned, "When people do not attempt to prevent an evil that they see before them, they should await Allaah's punishment." [Tirmidhi and Ibn Majah] Rasulullaah (sallAllaahu-alaihi-wasallam) is also reported to have said, "When people do not restrain the hand of an oppressor, they should await a widespread punishment from Allaah." [Abu Dawood]

Hadhrat Wahshi (R.A) was the person who killed Hadhrat Hamzah (R.A). When he intended to accept Islaam, he sent a letter to Rasulullaah (sallAllaahu-alaihi-wasallam) stating his intentions, but added that the following verse of the Qur'aan prevented him from doing so. The verse in question was, **"Those who do not subscribe to another deity with Allaah; do not kill those souls that Allaah has forbidden except**

with warrant; and do not commit adultery. Whoever perpetrates these shall be a sinner."

He wrote to say that he had perpetrated all these evils, so was there any Taubah (repentance) for him?

Allaah then revealed the verse, **"Except for him who repents, believes and does good actions."** Rasulullaah (sallAllaahu-alaihi-wasallam) had this written and sent to Hadhrat Wahshi (R.A).

He wrote back saying that the verse stipulates the performance of good actions and he did not know whether he would be able to comply.

Thereupon Allaah revealed the verse, **"Verily Allaah does not forgive that partners be ascribed unto Him, but forgives all besides this for whomsoever He wills."** This verse was also sent to him.

He again wrote back saying that this verse stipulates that Allaah will only forgive those whom He wills. He expressed doubt about whether Allaah would wish to forgive him or not.

Thereafter the verse was revealed declaring, **"Say, 'Oh My bondsmen who have transgressed against their souls! Do not be despondent of Allaah's mercy. Verily Allaah forgives all sins. Inaction He is the Most Forgiving, the Most Merciful."**

After this verse was sent to him, he arrived in Madinah to accept Islaam.

THE BEHAVIOR OF MAN IS STRANGE INDEED.

The following statement of Allaah's has been reported by Hadhrat Muhammad bin Mutarraf (R.A). Allaah says, "The behaviour of man is truly strange. He asks forgiveness from Me after sinning, and I forgive him. Then he sins again, asks for forgiveness, whereafter I forgive him once more. He neither refrains from sin, nor does he grow despondent of My mercy. Oh Angels! Be witness to the fact that I have forgiven them."

Note: Every sinner should continue to seek Allaah's forgiveness and must not persist in his sins. The penitent person will not be termed as one who is persistent in committing sins, even though he repents seventy times a day.

TAUBA IS ACCEPTED ONLY BEFORE DEATH.

Hadhrat Hasan Basri (R.A) reports that Rasulullaah (sallAllaahu-alaihi-wasallam) said, "When Allaah placed Iblees on the earth, he said to Allaah, 'By Your honour and grandeur! I shall continue in my attempts to mislead man as long as his soul remains in his body.' Allaah told him in reply, 'By My honour and grandeur! I shall continue to accept the repentance of man before he reaches the throes of death."

THE REMORSE AND DESPONDENCY OF THE ACCURSED IBLEES :- IN FIVES.

It has been reported that no sin of a person is recorded till these reach five. Thereafter, if he does five good actions, five rewards are recorded in his account and the five sins are obliterated thereby. Iblees then laments with despondency, "How can I get man in my control when a single good actions destroys all my efforts?"

SIX QUALITIES OF ONE WHO TRULY RECOGNIZES ALLAAH.

1. When he remembers Allaah, he appreciates this boon.
2. When he looks at himself, he considers himself low. (Allaah's worship   is perfection in itself).
3. He takes a lesson from Allaah's signs. (This is his objective).
4. When the thoughts of passion and sin enters his mind, he becomes afraid. (Fearing the thought of sin is a sign of perfection).
5. He becomes happy when thinking about Allaah's attribute of forgiveness. (The salvation of man depends on Allaah's forgiveness).
6. He repents whenever he thinks about his sins.

THE EMINENT FUDAIL (R.A).

A group of highway robbers, whose leader was Hadhrat Fudail (R.A) once decided to waylay a caravan consisting of traders, travellers, aged people, women and children. They mounted their horses, brandished their swords and left to accost the caravan at a place where they had halted to rest.

When the band of robbers arrived, the people of the caravan dispersed in such frenzy that the scene was reminiscent of Qiyamah, with every person worrying about himself only. Mothers were screaming, children were wailing and the robbers were exploiting the situation with their usual cold heartedness.

In this confession, Hadhrat Fudail (R.A) came across a person in one section of the caravan who was busy reciting something. He approached the person in a fit of fury because the man was totally unafraid and unperturbed by their presence. As he drew closer to the person, he heard him recite the verse of the Qur'aan; **"Has the time not come for the believers that their hearts submit (and tremble) with the dhikr of Allaah?"** [Surah Haaction]

The glory of the Qur'aan is such that a few verses of Surah TaaHaa was enough to alter the image of Abu Hafs, Umar bin Khattaab into Hadhrat Umar (R.A). It then raised him to such a mantle that Rasulullaah (sallAllaahu-alaihi-wasallam) said, "If there was another prophet after me, it would have been Umar."

Similarly the words of the Quraan had such an impact upon Hadhrat Fudail (R.A), that he immediately threw down his sword, left his horse where it stood and ran into the forest leaving his henchmen behind. There he wept uncontrollably over all his past sins.

After a few days, another caravan was passing. The inmates, afraid of coming being attacked, asked one pious man in the vicinity whether Fudail was nearby or whether he was out plundering another caravan? The pious person told them not to be afraid of Fudail because he was now even scared of children.

Thereafter, Hadhrat Fudail (R.A) travelled from town to town looking for all those whom he had robbed. He then returned their property to them and sought forgiveness from them.

Allaah says in Surah Shams, **"Allaah has inspired evil and good in every soul. The one who purifies the soul is successful and the one who destroys it has certainly lost."**

TAUBATUN NASOOHA (SINCERE REPENTANCE):-
3 SIGNS.

Hadhrat Abdullaah bin Abbaas (R.A) interprets Taubatun Nasooh as when:

1. A person's heart is ashamed.
2. His tongue seeks forgiveness.
3. He resolves never to repeat the sin he comitted.

Allaah instructs us in Surah Tahreem, **"Oh you who believe, repent to Allaah, a sincere repentance (Taubatun Nasooha)."**

THE RESOLUTION NOT TO REPEAT A SIN IS IMPERATIVE WHEN ONE REPENTS.

Rasulullaah (sallAllaahu-alaihi-wasallam) said, "The example of the person who repents and then continues to sin is like that of one who tries to make a fool of Allaah."

A UNIQUE STORY.

One of the kings of the Bani Isra'eel employed a particular slave in his service after hearing much praise of him. Seeing the king in a good mood, the slave asked him, "What will be your reaction if you walked into your palace one day and had to see me engaged in joking and merrymaking with one of your concubines?" The king was enraged and cursed the slave for his impudence. The slave bid the king to be calm and told him that he was merely testing him. He then said to the king, "I am the slave of such a Master who never gets as angry as you do despite seeing His slave sin seventy times a day. He neither hits me for it, nor does He deprive me of my sustenance (instead, He forgives me when I repent). Why should I leave him for you. I have just now experienced your reaction to an imaginary situation. What will your reaction be when one really disobeys you?"

SHAYTAAN ALSO HAS REGRETS.

A taabi'ee has mentioned that when a sinner repents for his sins and is remorseful of, his ranks are elevated even more and he becomes worthy of Jannah. It is then that shaytaan lamentingly says, "If I had only not encouraged him to sin (then his ranks would not have been raised)!"

HASTE IS BEST IN THREE THINGS.

1. Salaah, when the time sets in.
2. The burial of a deceased person.
3. Repentance after a sin (it should not be that he dies without repenting).

THE SIGNS OF TAUBA.

Certain wise men have mentioned that acceptance of Tauba can be recognized by four signs. These are:

1. A person guards his tongue from futile talk, lying and backbiting.
2. He harbours no jealousy or enmity for anyone.
3. He forsakes evil company.
4. He prepares for death, is always remorseful, always repenting and always obedient to Allaah's orders.

A wise man was once asked, "Are there any signs whereby it can be recognized that a person's Tauba is accepted?" He replied that there were the following four signs:

1. He disassociates from the company of evil people and joins the company of good people, having true reverence for them in his heart.
2. He disassociates from all sins and turns to good actions only.
3. He removes the love of the world from his heart and is constantly worried about the Hereafter.
4. He remains unworried about his sustenance, which Allaah has assumed responsibility for, and engages in Allaah's obedience.

People owe the following four responsibilities to such a person:

1. They should love him because Allaah loves him.
2. They should pray that Allaah keeps him constant on Taubah.
3. They should not taunt him about his previous sins.
4. They should remain in his company, talk about him and assist him in every way.

FOUR HONOR THAT ALLAAH CONFERS UPON ONE WHO REPENTS.

Allaah honours him with four things viz.

1. Allaah purifies him for sins in such a manner that it is as if he had never committed any sin.
2. Allaah begins to love him.
3. Allaah protects him from shaytaan.
4
5. Allaah makes him fearless and content before he leaves the world.

THE FIRE OF JAHANNAM WILL NOT AFFECT THE REPENTANT PERSON AS HE CROSSES OVER IT.

Hadhrat Khaalid bin Ma'daan (R.A) says that when the repentant people will enter Jannah, they will ask, "Allaah has mentioned that we will have to cross over Jahannam before entering Jannah?" They will be told that they have already passed over Jahannam, but it was cooled (for them).

THE WARNING AGAINST TAUNTING A MUSLIM.

Rasulullaah (sallAllaahu-alaihi-wasallam) has mentioned, "The Muslim who taunts another Muslim due to any evil, thereby embarrassing him, shall be just like the one who committed the evil (i.e. it will be as if he perpetrated the sin himself). The person who defames a Mu'min on account of any of his sins shall be involved in the same sin and defamation before he dies." (May Allaah save us therefrom).

Faqeeh Abul Laith (R.A) says that a Mu'min never sins intentionally. His sins are always due to negligence and he is then forgiven after he repents. Therefore, why should he be taunted?

SINS ARE TOTALLY OBLITERATED BY TAUBA.

Hadhrat Abdullah bin Abbaas (R.A) reports that when a slave repents to Allaah, Allaah forgives him and causes the recording angels as well as the person's limbs to forget about the sin. Therefore, they are unable to testify against him. Even the ground whereupon the sin was committed forgets the sin.

When Allaah cursed shaytaan he swore by Allaah honour that he will never leave the bosom of man. Allaah then swore by His honour that He would forgive man as long as he lives.

THE EXCELLENCE OF THE UMMAH OF Rasulullaah (sallAllaahu-alaihi-wasallam).

The Tauba of the previous ummahs (nations) was that Allaah made a halaal thing haraam due to their sins. Allaah also used to write their sin on their doors or on their limbs.

However, Allaah has been extremely bountiful to the ummah of Rasulullaah (sallAllaahu-alaihi-wasallam) by not exposing their sins in this manner.

Whenever the sinner turns to Allaah asking for forgiveness, Allaah says, "My slave has sinned and has realized that he has a Rabb Who is Forgiving and Who has the power to take him to task." Allaah then forgives the person.

Allaah says, **"Whoever commits a sin or oppresses himself, and then seeks forgiveness from Allaah, he shall find Allaah to be Most Forgiving, Most Merciful."** A person should repent every morning and evening for his sins.

GOOD ACTIONS ARE AWAITED BEFORE A SIN IS RECORDED:- 5 SINS.

Every person has an angel on each shoulder, who records his actions. The angel on the right shoulder is the leader. Whenever the angel on the left shoulder intends to record a sin that is committed, the angel on the right stops him saying, "Do not write until five sins are committed."

When five sins are perpetrated, the angel on the left requests permission to write. He is again prevented from writing with the words, "Wait. Perchance he may carry out a good action." When the person does carry out a good action, the angel on the right says, "Allaah has stipulated the principle that every good action will earn the reward of ten actions. Therefore this person has earned the reward of ten good actions for his one act. Since his sins are five, they will be forgiven in lieu of five actions and I shall record five good actions in his account."

It is then that shaytaan wails as he says, "How can I ever gain control over man?"

SINS ARE TRANSFORMED INTO GOOD ACTIONS BY VIRTUE OF TAUBA.

Hadhrat Abu Huraira (R.A) reports that he was once walking with Rasulullaah (sallAllaahu-alaihi-wasallam) after Isha. On the road a woman asked, "Oh Abu Huraira! I have perpetrated a sin. How can I secure forgiveness?" When Hadhrat Abu Huraira (R.A) enquired about the sin, she said that she had committed adultery and killed the illegitimate child born therefrom.

Realizing the gravity of the sin, Hadhrat Abu Huraira (R.A) told her, "You are destroyed and have destroyed another as well. How can you be forgiven?" Hearing this she fell unconscious. Hadhrat Abu Huraira (R.A) continued ahead, but remained remorseful, thinking that he should enquire from Rasulullaah (sallAllaahu-alaihi-wasallam) about the matter.

The following morning, when he informed Rasulullaah (sallAllaahu-alaihi-wasallam) about the incident, Rasulullaah (sallAllaahu-alaihi-wasallam) said, "Inna Lillahi wa Inna Ilayhi Raji'oon (To Allaah we belong and to Him shall we return. Abu Huraira! You have destroyed yourself and another. Have you not read the verse of the Qur'aan where Allaah says, **"Those who do not subscribe to another deity with Allaah, do not kill those souls that Allaah has forbidden except with warrant, and do not commit adultery. Whoever perpetrates these shall be a sinner. Punishment will be doubled for them on the Day of Qiyamah, and they will remain therein forever. Except for him who repents, believes and does good actions. For these people Allaah will convert their sins into good actions. Allaah is ever the Most Forgiving, the Most Merciful."**

Hadhrat Abu Huraira (R.A) says that he then roamed through all the streets of Madinah in search of this woman, announcing, "Where is the woman who asked me a ruling last night?" Seeing his condition, the children said that he must be mad.

That night he met the woman at the same place. He told her what Rasulullaah (sallAllaahu-alaihi-wasallam) had said adding that the doors of repentance were open for her. She was so overcome with joy that she donated a certain orchard of hers to the poor.

Ulama have mentioned that sins are replaced by correspondingly proportional good actions. Allaah is even prepared to forgive kufr. He says, **"Tell the disbelievers, 'If they repent from kufr, they will be forgiven for all that has past."**

If kufr, which is a terrible sin, can be forgiven, others must surely be forgivable.

THE STATEMENT OF HADHRAT MOOSA (A.S).

Hadhrat Moosa (A.S) said, "Astonishing is that person who laughs, despite being convinced about Jahannam; who is happy, despite being convinced of death; who sins, despite being convinced of reckoning; who grieves, despite being convinced of Taqdeer (fate); who is content with the world, despite witnessing it's changes; and the one who does not carry out good actions, despite his conviction in Jannah."

THE REPENTANCE OF ZAAZAAN.

Hadhrat Abdullah bin Mas'ood (R.A) was once passing through a place where people were intoxicated with liquor and a person named Zaazaan was singing to them in an extremely melodious voice. Hadhrat Abdullah bin Mas'ood (R.A) said, "What a beautiful voice. If it was only used to recite the Qur'aan, it would truly be appreciated." He then covered his head with a shawl and left.

Zaazaan noticed him and asked the people about who he was and what he had said. The people informed him that it was Hadhrat Abdullah bin Mas'ood (R.A), who was a companion of Rasulullaah (sallAllaahu-alaihi-wasallam). They also told him what he had said. Hearing this, Zaazaan was taken aback. He immediately broke his drum and ran weeping after Hadhrat Abdullah bin Mas'ood (R.A).

Hadhrat Abdullah bin Mas'ood (R.A) hugged him and they both began to cry. Hadhrat Abdullah bin Mas'ood (R.A) then mentioned, "Why should I not love the person whom Allaah loves?" Zaazaan then repented and learnt the Qur'aan from Hadhrat Abdullah bin Mas'ood (R.A). He attained such proficiency in the Qur'aan and in other Islaamic sciences that he became a learned scholar of the time. Numerous narrations of Ahadeeth record him as a narrator from Hadhrat Abdullah bin Mas'ood (R.A).

A THOUGHT PROVOKING INCIDENT.

Faqeeh Abul Laith (R.A) narrates that his father used to recount the incident of an extremely beautiful woman from the Bani Isra'eel, who used to ensnare men into fornication. Her door remained open at all times and men would be attracted when they saw her sitting there. She would charge them a fee of ten gold coins to do as they pleased with her.

Incidentally a saint once passed by her house. He was immediately infatuated when he set eyes on her and could not fight the temptation to have her. He made du'a to Allaah and tried to convince himself to discard of the evil, but the flames could not be doused. Eventually, he sold of his belongings and collected ten gold coins. She instructed him to hand the money over to her solicitor, and an appointment was duly fixed for him.

When he arrived at her home, he found that she had adorned herself well and looked stunning. When he stretched out his hand to touch her, Allaah's grace and the blessings of his worship caused an uncontrollable fear to grip his heart. It then occurred to him that Allaah was watching his vile act. His gaze then dropped, his hands trembled and his face grew pale. The woman had never seen such a sight before and asked him what was wrong. He replied, "I fear my Rabb. Please allow me to leave."

She said, "Shame be on you. You are afraid and want to leave when you have the desire of thousands of men before you! What is this all about?" He said, "It is nothing. Just allow me to leave and I will not even ask for a refund of my money." She said, "Could this perhaps be the first time in your life?"

When he replied in the affirmative, she allowed him to leave on condition that he leaves his name and address with her. He complied and then left her, shouting and cursing himself and throwing sand on his head due to remorse.

As he left, the woman began to reconsider her situation. She thought that this person became so overcome with Allaah's fear whereas he had only intended to sin for the first time in his life. She, on the other hand, had spent so many years actually perpetrating the act, yet her Rabb was the same as his. She realized that she should fear Allaah even more. She then repented for her sins, shut the door, removed her beautiful clothing and wore old and tattered clothing.

It then occurred to her to learn from a saint, without whom she would not be able to rid herself of her faults. She decided to search for the same man, thinking that he may marry her and teach her about the Deen. Consequently, she gathered a considerable amount of her animals and wealth, and left in search of the saint. After many inquiries, she located him in a village. When she removed her veil before him, he gave a shout and immediately passed away.

She was left standing there in astonishment. She then enquired from the people whether he had any unmarried relatives. They informed her of his brother, who was extremely poor, but exceptionally pious. She declared that she had no use for her wealth and consequently married the brother. The couple had seven sons, all of whom were accorded lofty ranks by Allaah. **"Such is the grace of Allaah that He accords to whom He wills."**

A HADITH QUDSI:- 9 ADVICES.

Hadhrat Abu Dharr (R.A) narrates from Rasulullaah (sallAllaahu-alaihi-wasallam) that Allaah says:

- ☙ Oh My slaves! Just as I have forbidden oppression upon Myself, you should also consider it haraam to oppress others.
- ☙ Oh My slaves! You were all once astray except for those whom I had guided. Therefore, ask Me for guidance and I shall guide you.

- Oh My slaves! All of you were hungry save for those whom I had fed. Therefore, ask Me for sustenance, and I will provide for you.
- Oh My slaves! All of you were naked, save those whom I had clothed. Therefore, ask Me for clothing and I will provide it for you.

- Oh My slaves! You are constantly engaged in sins, but I conceal our sins for you. Therefore, seek forgiveness only from Me and I will certainly forgive you.
- Oh My slaves! You can neither be of benefit to Me , nor can you harm Me.
- Oh My slaves! If all your past and future generations of man and jinn collectively become extremely pious, it will not add an iota to My sovereignty.
- Oh My slaves! If all your past and future generations of man and jinn collectively become extremely evil, it will not decrease an iota from My sovereignty.
- Oh My slaves! If all of man and jinn from the time of Hadhrat Aadam (A.S) have to gather at a place and ask from Me, and if I then had to fulfill every desire of each individual, it would not even decrease from My treasures the amount that decreases from the ocean when a pin is dipped therein and removed.

SERVING ONE'S PARENTS IS SUPERIOR THAN JIHAAD.

A Sahabi (R.A) once requested permission from Rasulullaah (sallAllaahu-alaihi-wasallam) to fight in jihaad. When Rasulullaah (sallAllaahu-alaihi-wasallam) asked him whether his parents were alive, he replied in the affirmative. Rasulullaah (sallAllaahu-alaihi-wasallam) then told him, "Go and strive in their service."

When even an able man is not required to fight in jihaad, it will be better for a person to rather serve his parents at home. He may not proceed for jihaad without their permission. The least form of disobedience to parents is to mutter a word like "Uff!" when displeased about something.

Allaah says, **"Do not even say 'Uff!' to them and do not reproach them."**

THREE ACTIONS ARE NOT ACCEPTED WITHOUT ANOTHER THREE.

It has been mentioned that three verses of the Qur'aan cannot be practiced upon without practicing on both the constituents of each verse. These are:

1. **"Establish salaah and pay zakaah."** Salaah will not be accepted without paying zakaah and vice versa. (Of course, this will only apply to the wealthy people upon whom zakaah is obligatory.
2. **"Obey Allaah and obey the Rasul (messenger)."** Allaah cannot be obeyed without Rasulullaah (sallAllaahu-alaihi-wasallam) and vice versa.
3. **"Show gratitude to Me and your parents."** A person cannot be grateful to Allaah without being grateful to his parents and vice versa. The person who pleases his parents pleases Allaah and the one who displeases his parents displeases Allaah.

Hadhrat Farkhad Sabkhi (R.A) says that he read in a book that it is not befitting of children to even talk without the permission of their parents. They should only speak when asked something and should never walk in front, on the right, or on the left of their parents. They must always walk behind them.

DISPLEASING ONE'S PARENTS RESULTS IN A BAD DEATH.

Hadhrat Anas (R.A) reports that there was a person during the time of Rasulullaah (sallAllaahu-alaihi-wasallam) by the name of Alqama (R.A). He exerted himself greatly for the Deen and gave a lot of charity. It once happened that he fell seriously ill. His wife summoned Rasulullaah (sallAllaahu-alaihi-wasallam) via another woman.

Rasulullaah (sallAllaahu-alaihi-wasallam) sent Hadhrat Ali, Bilaal, Salmaan Faarsi and Ammaar (R.A) to examine the situation. They found Hadhrat Alqama (R.A) in the throes of death and, try as they may, they could not get him to recite the kalimah. Hadhrat Bilaal (R.A) reported the situation to Rasulullaah (sallAllaahu-alaihi-wasallam).

Rasulullaah (sallAllaahu-alaihi-wasallam) asked whether the parents of Hadhrat Alqama (R.A) were alive. Rasulullaah (sallAllaahu-alaihi-wasallam) was informed that his mother was alive, and that she was extremely old. Rasulullaah (sallAllaahu-alaihi-wasallam) sent Hadhrat Bilaal (R.A) to request her to come to him, otherwise he would go to her.

When the old lady received the message, she said, "May my soul be sacrificed for Rasulullaah (sallAllaahu-alaihi-wasallam)! I shall go to him." She then took the support of a stick and walked to meet Rasulullaah (sallAllaahu-alaihi-wasallam). When she arrived in the presence of Rasulullaah (sallAllaahu-alaihi-wasallam), she greeted with salaam and sat down.

Rasulullaah (sallAllaahu-alaihi-wasallam) replied to her greeting and told her, "Do reply truthfully to whatever I shall ask you. If you lie, I will be informed thereof by revelation. Tell me. What kind of a person is Alqama?" She replied, "He performs a lot of salaah, fasts often and his spending in charity cannot even be estimated."

Rasulullaah (sallAllaahu-alaihi-wasallam) then asked her, "How is the relationship between the two of you?" She replied, "I am angry with him." When Rasulullaah (sallAllaahu-alaihi-wasallam) asked her the reason for this, she said, "Because he gives preference to his wife over me. He listens to her more than he listens to me and accepts what she has to say."

Rasulullaah (sallAllaahu-alaihi-wasallam) said, "The displeasure of his mother as prevented him from reciting the kalimah." Turning to Hadhrat Bilaal (R.A), Rasulullaah (sallAllaahu-alaihi-wasallam) said, "Bilaal! Gather some wood so that I may burn Alqama." The old lady was startled and asked, "Oh Rasulullaah (sallAllaahu-alaihi-wasallam)! Are you going to burn my son, the apple of my eye? How can I tolerate this?"

Rasulullaah (sallAllaahu-alaihi-wasallam) told her, "Allaah's punishment is more severe and eternal. If you wish that Allaah forgives your son then be pleased with him. By Allaah! His salaah, fasting, etc can never be of avail without your pleasure." She immediately raised her hands and said, "Oh Rasulullaah (sallAllaahu-alaihi-wasallam)! I call yourself and all those present here to witness that I am pleased with Alqama!"

Rasulullaah (sallAllaahu-alaihi-wasallam) then sent Hadhrat Bilaal (R.A) to see whether Alqama (R.A) could recite the kalimah. He said, "It is just possible that she has declared her pleasure with Alqama because of me, without being pleased with him from her heart." As Hadhrat Bilaal (R.A) entered the door, he heard Hadhrat Alqama (R.A) loudly reciting, "Laa ilaaha IllAllaah." Hadhrat Bilaal (R.A) told the people that the displeasure of Alqama's mother had handicapped his tongue.

Hadhrat Alqama (R.A) passed away the same day. Rasulullaah (sallAllaahu-alaihi-wasallam) performed the funeral (Janazah) salaah and then told the people, "Listen, Oh gathering of Muhajireen and Ansaar! Allaah's curse is on the person who prefers his wife to his mother. Neither are his Faraaidh nor his Nawaafil accepted."

CHILDREN OWE TEN RIGHTS TO THEIR PARENTS.

1. They should be provided with food if they do not have any.
2. They should be given clothing if they do not possess any.
3. They should be served if necessary.
4. If they call, they should be immediately attended to.
5. They should be gently spoken to and never addressed harshly.
6. They must never be called by their names since this is disrespectful.
7. Children should walk behind them and never in front of them, nor by their sides.
8. One should like for them what he likes for himself and dislike for them what he dislikes for himself.
9. One should always make du'a for them. By not making du'a for them, a person's life will be straitened.
10. Every command of theirs should be duly obeyed, unless it contradicts the sharia (Law of Allaah).

PLEASING THE PARENTS AFTER THEIR DEATH:- BY 3 THINGS.

Children can please their parents by doing three things after the demise of the parents. These are:

1. The children should be pious. This will bring them more pleasure than anything else.
2. The children should maintain good relations with the family and friends of their deceased parents.

3. They should make du'a for the forgiveness of their parents and give charity on their behalf.

PARENTS OWE THREE RIGHTS TO THEIR CHILDREN.

Rasulullaah (sallAllaahu-alaihi-wasallam) mentioned that parents owe three rights to their children. These are:

1. Giving them good names (that have good meanings).
2. Teaching them the Qur'aan when they are of an understanding age.
3. Marrying them off when they come of age.

THE CONSEQUENCE OF NOT TEACHING CHILDREN GOOD MANNERS.

A person complained to Hadhrat Abu Hafs Sikandari (R.A) that his son hit him. Hadhrat Abu Hafs (R.A) exclaimed, "SubhaanAllaah! A son hitting his father! Did he really hit you? Did you teach your son manners and respect?"

"No," replied the father. "Did you teach him the Qur'aan?" was the next question. Again that reply was in the negative. Abu Hafs (R.A) then asked the father what the occupation of his son was. The father replied that he was a farmer.

"Do you know why he hit you?" asked Hadhrat Abu Hafs (R.A). When the father could not give a reply, Abu Hafs (R.A) told him, "It seems to me that he rides a donkey to work every morning. A bull walks in front of him and a dog behind. Since you did not teach him the Qur'aan, which he could recite on the way, he must be singing as he proceeds. You must have tried to stop him from singing, so he considered you to be a bull, and hit you. You should thank Allaah that he did not fracture your head."

AS YOU SOW, SO SHALL YOU REAP.

Hadhrat Thaabit Banaani (R.A) says that someone made mention of a person who was hitting his father. When someone intervened, they father told him, "Do not intervene and do not say anything because I used to hit my father at this same spot. I am therefore receiving my punishment. It is no fault of my son, so do not scold him."

PERFECT POLITENESS :- REAPS 8 BENEFITS.

Hadhrat Fudail bin Ayaadh (R.A) says that the person with perfect politeness is one who:

1. Obeys his parents.
2. Maintains sound family ties.
3. Serves his friends.
4. Is courteous towards his wife, servants and employees.
5. Safeguards his Deen.
6. Is careful with his wealth and only spends where necessary.
7. Guards his tongue.
8. Spends most of his time at home, avoiding wasting time on futile gatherings.

THE FOUR SIGNS OF GOOD FORTUNE.

Rasulullaah (sallAllaahu-alaihi-wasallam) said that four things denote the good fortune of a person. These are:

1. His wife is pious.
2. His children are obedient and pious.
3. His partners and associates are pious.
4. His sustenance is found within his town.

THE REWARDS OF FIVE THINGS WILL CONTINUE TO BE RECEIVED EVEN AFTER DEATH.

Hadhrat Anas (R.A) has mentioned that the rewards of five things will continue to be received even after death viz.

1. The digging of a well (or another water source,untill it is depleted).
2. Building of a Masjid (as long as people engage in worship therein)
3. Writing the Qur'aan (as long as people read from it).
4. An orchard (or tree, as long as people derive benefit therefrom).

5. Pious children or students (the father or teacher will continue to benefit from these products of theirs).

SOME AHADEETH.

ᛆ Hadhrat Abu Huraira (R.A) narrates that Rasulullaah (sallAllaahu-alaihi-wasallam) said, "May he be disgraced! May he be disgraced! May he be disgraced! The person whose parents, or any one of them, reach old age and he does not attain Jannah (by serving them)." [Muslim]

ᛆ Hadhrat Abdullaah bin Mas'ood (R.A) reports that he once asked Rasulullaah (sallAllaahu-alaihi-wasallam), "Which action is most beloved to Allaah?" Rasulullaah (sallAllaahu-alaihi-wasallam) replied, "Salaah during it's time." He then asked, "What next?" The reply was, "Kindness to parents." When he asked what was next in merit, Rasulullaah (sallAllaahu-alaihi-wasallam) said, "Jihaad in Allaah's way." [Bukhari and Muslim]

Rasulullaah (sallAllaahu-alaihi-wasallam) has mentioned, "No action receives reward faster than the maintenance of good family ties and no action attracts punishment faster than the severance of family ties."

THREE QUALITIES OF THE PEOPLE OF JANNAH

The following are three qualities that are found in the people of Jannah and are exclusive to those who are noble an honourable. They are:

- Being good to those who are bad to them.
- Forgiving those who oppress them.
- Spending on those who do not give anything to them.

A STATEMENT OF HADHRAT UMAR (R.A).

"By adopting taqwa and maintaining sound family ties one's life is extended, sustenance is blessed, and mutual love grows."

MUSLIMS AND KUFFAR ARE TO BE TREATED EQUALLY IN THREE RESPECTS.

Hadhrat Maymoon bin Mihraan (R.A) says that Muslims and the kuffar must be treated equally in three respects viz.

1. In the fulfillment of promises pledged to them.
2. In the maintenance of good family relations.
3. In returning of trusts in the same condition as they were received.

A STATEMENT OF HADHRAT HASAN BASRI (R.A).

Allaah's curse is on those people who display knowledge, but destroy action, who express love with the tongue, while the heart harbours hatred, and who sever family ties.

Faqeeh Abul Laith (R.A) says that it is compulsory to send gifts and regularly meet those relatives who live close by. If one is unable to give gifts, then he should at least meet with them and render them assistance when need be. If they live in a distant place, one must write to them in an effort to maintain ties.

TEN BENEFITS OF FOSTERING GOOD FAMILY RELATIONS.

1. It harnesses Allaah's pleasure.
2. It pleases the relative (pleasing a Mu'min is a form of worship).
3. It pleases the angels.
4. It earns the praises of others (which is a bounty if it is not made one's objective).
5. It grieves Iblees.
6. It increases one's lifespan (The life is more blessed and one earns more reward because he has time to do more good actions).
7. It increases the blessings in one's sustenance.
8. It even pleases the deceased (when they are informed thereof).
9. It increases peoples' love for one (they will therefore be ready to assist one at the time of need).

10. The reward earned thereby continues to accrue to one even after his death (those with whom one maintained good ties will continue to make du'a for him after his demise).

THREE GROUPS OF PEOPLE WILL BE BENEATH THE SHADE OF ALLAAH'S THRONE ON THE DAY OF QIYAMAH.

Hadhrat Anas bin Maalik (R.A) say that three groups of people will be beneath the shade of Allaah's throne on the Day of Judgement viz.

1. Those who fostered good family ties (since he comforted people in this world, Allaah will see to his comfort on the Day of Qiyamah by shading him and protecting him from the torment of that day).
2. Those widows who did not remarry for the sake of their children.
3. Those who also invited orphans and poor people to a feast.

ALLAAH LOVES TWO FOOTSTEPS.

Rasulullaah (sallAllaahu-alaihi-wasallam) has mentioned that Allaah loves two footsteps very much. The first is the footstep taken towards salaah, and the second is the one taken in the direction of joining family ties.

FIVE FACTORS THAT INFLATE THE REWARDS OF ACTIONS TO THE SIZE OF MOUNTAINS AND INCREASES ONE'S SUSTENANCE.

1. To inculcate the habit of spending in charity (irrespective of the amount).
2. Fostering sound family relations (to any degree).
3. To continuously strive in Allaah's path (in any form).
4. To always remain in the state of wudhu.
5. To obey the parents at all times and in all circumstances.

Spending in charity, maintaining family ties and obeying one's parents are of the highest forms of fulfilling the rights of people. Striving in Allaah's path is one of the highest forms of fulfilling Allaah's rights. Constantly remaining in the state of wudhu is the best way of averting shaytaan's plots and other calamities.

SOME AHADEETH.

ชช Rasulullaah (sallAllaahu-alaihi-wasallam) said, "Whoever believes in Allaah and the last day should entertain his guest. Whoever believes in Allaah and the last day should join family ties. Whoever believes in Allaah and the last day should speak what is good or remain silent." [Bukhari and Muslim]

ﻭ Rasulullaah (sallAllaahu-alaihi-wasallam) said, "The person who yearns that his sustenance and his life be blessed, should maintain good family ties."

ﻭ Rasulullaah (sallAllaahu-alaihi-wasallam) has mentioned, "The proper maintainer of amily ties is not the one who treats others as they do to him, but he is one who joins with those who sever ties with him."

7 TYPES OF PEOPLE UPON WHOM THERE IS NO MERCY.

Faqeeh Abul Laith Samarqandi (R.A) has reported from Rasulullaah (sallAllaahu-alaihi-wasallam) that Allaah will not look with mercy towards seven types of people, and He will enter them into Jahannam. These are:

1. Both parties involved in an act of sodomy.
2. Those who masturbate.
3. Those who sodomise animals.
4. Those who engage in anal sex.
5. Those who marry a mother and a daughter.
6. Those who commit adultery with their neighbours' wives.
7. Those who harass and cause inconvenience to their neighbours.

All these categories of people are deserving of Allaah's curse till they repent sincerely.

Rasulullaah (sallAllaahu-alaihi-wasallam) has mentioned that no person can be a perfect Mu'min till people are safe from his hands and tongue. Similarly no person can be a perfect Mu'min till his neighbour is safe from his evil.

9 RIGHTS ON A NEIGHBOUR

A person once asked Rasulullaah (sallAllaahu-alaihi-wasallam), "What are the rights of a neighbour?" The reply was:

1. He should be granted a loan upon request.
2. His invitation should be accepted.
3. He should be visited when ill.
4. He should be assisted upon request.

5. He should be consoled when he suffers any loss.
6. He should be congratulated upon a happy occasion.
7. His funeral should be attended.
8. His home and family should be cared for in his absence.
9. A high building should not be constructed without his permission.

5 WORDS OF WISDOM.

Rasulullaah (sallAllaahu-alaihi-wasallam) advised Hadhrat Abu Huraira (R.A) thus:

1. Adopt abstinence and you will be considered as one who worships the most.
2. Be content and you will be regarded as the most grateful.
3. Like for others what you like for yourself and you will be a perfect Mu'min.
4. Treat your neighbours well and you will be a perfect Muslim.
5. Laugh less because excessive laughter kills the heart.

THREE TYPES OF NEIGHBOURS.

Rasulullaah (sallAllaahu-alaihi-wasallam) has mentioned that there are three kinds of neighbours viz.
(1) the one with three rights,
(2) the one with two rights and
(3) the one with one right.

The first type is that neighbour who is a Muslim, a relative and a neighbour.
The second is he who is a Muslim and neighbour, who is not a relative. The third type is the non-Muslim, who is only a neighbour.

THREE ADVICES.

Hadhrat Abu Dharr Ghifaari (R.A) says that his beloved friend, Rasulullaah (sallAllaahu-alaihi-wasallam) gave him three advices. These were:

1. Obey the leader even though his nose may be cut off (when his command does not contradict the sharia).
2. Add more water to your gravy so that you could give some to your neighbour.
3. Perform salaah on it's due time.

A FEW PEARLS OF WISDOM.

⅄ Hadhrat Hasan Basri (R.A) says, "Good behaviour towards neighbours does not only mean that one does not cause any harm to them. it also includes being patient when they harm you."

⅄ Hadhrat Amr bin Al Aas (R.A) has mentioned, "Maintaining good family ties does not mean that a person joins ties with those who joins ties with him, and severes ties with those who sever ties with him. This is equity. Proper maintenance of ties means that you join ties with those who sever them and that you behave well with those who oppress and harass you. Sin ilarly, forbearance does not mean that you are forbearing with those who are forbearing towards you and that you behave foolishly with those who behave foolishly towards you. This is also mere equity. True forbearance is when you are patient with the foolishness of fools and the harassment of neighbours. Not harassing them is best."

THE POSITION OF A NEIGHBOUR.

That neighbour is best, who is trusted by his neighbours in every respect and who never says anything that has to be retracted if his neighbour has to appear, that will be a cause of embarrassment if the neighbour has to learn of it.

A good neighbour is also him who the other neighbour trusts so much that he feels assured that any valuable will not be touched in his absence (neither will the neighbour himself touch it, nor will he allow others to do so). It becomes then easy for the neighbour to leave something in his custody.

THREE PRAISEWORTHY TRAITS DURING THE PERIOD OF IGNORANCE.

Hadhrat Abdullah bin Abbaas (R.A) says, "Three qualities were practiced during the period of ignorance. Muslims are more worthy of acting on these. These are:

1. Entertaining guests.
2. Not divorcing wives who have aged so that they do not experience any difficulties in their old age.
3. If a person was in debt, all his neighbours would contribute towards paying off his debt. They would also assist him in any other difficulty.

THE POOR NEIGHBOUR WILL CALL THE RICH NEIGHBOUR TO TASK.

Rasulullaah (sallAllaahu-alaihi-wasallam) has mentioned, "On the Day of Judgement a person will grab hold of his neighbour saying, "Oh Allaah! You made him rich, while I was poor. There were nights when I slept on an empty stomach, while he would go to bed with a full stomach every night. Ask him why he closed his door on me and why he deprived me of the wealth that You blessed him with."

TEN OPPRESSORS.

Hadhrat Sufyaan Thauri (R.A) says that ten people are regarded as oppressors viz.

1. The person who prays for himself, but forget his parents and other Mu'mineen.
2. The person who does not recite at least a hundred verses of the Qur'aan daily.
3. The person who leaves the Masjid without performing at least two rakaahs of salaah.
4. The person who passes a graveyard without greeting the deceased or praying for them.
5. The person who enters a city on a Friday and leaves without performing the Jumu'ah salaah.
6. That man or woman in whose vicinity a learned person comes and none acquires any religious knowledge from him.
7. Those two people who love each other for the pleasure of Allaah but are unaware of each others names.
8. That person who is invited by another but does not accept his invitation (when acceptance does not contradict the shari'ah).
9. That youngster that has no commitments yet does not acquire any religious knowledge or manners.
10. That person who has eaten to his fill while his neighbour goes hungry.

FOUR WAYS WHEREBY GOOD RELATIONS MAY BE MAINTAINED WITH ONE'S NEIGHBOUR.

Faqeeh Abul Laith Samarqandi (R.A) said perfect relations may be maintained with a neighbour in four ways viz.

1. To assist the neighbour with whatever means are at one's disposal.
2. Never desire that which your neighbour possesses.
3. Never harm your neighbour in any way.
4. Exercise patience when your neighbour causes you any difficulty.

Rasulullaah (sallAllaahu-alaihi-wasallam) said, "Make it incumbent upon yourself because truthfulness is piety and piety leads to Jannah. A person endeavours to be truthful and continues to do so till Allaah records him in the list of the truthful. Abstain from lying because it constitutes sin and vice, which leads one to Jahannam. A person continues to lie until he is recorded in the list of liars."

A SAYING OF HADHRAT LUQMAAN (A.S).

Someone asked Hadhrat Lumaan (A.S), "How did you achieve this high rank?" He replied, "By means of truthfulness, trustworthiness and abstaining from futility."

SIX THINGS GUARANTEE JANNAH.

Rasulullaah (sallAllaahu-alaihi-wasallam) said, "Guarantee six things for me and I will guarantee Jannah for you in exchange viz.

1. Always speak the truth.
2. Fulfill promises to the best of your ability.
3. Do not betray anyone's trust.
4. Protect your private organs.
5. Keep your gazes lowered.
6. Restrain your hands from oppression."

Truthfulness, fulfilling of promises and guarding trusts are all actions that relate to Allaah and man as well. Truthfulness to Allaah means that a person admits to Allaah's Oneness and recites the Kalimah with sincerity. Saying anything untrue constitutes lying to people, and cannot be condoned.

It is also compulsory for people to fulfill the pledge that they took with Allaah before time (i.e. the pledge to accept Allaah as their Rabb.) As far as possible, man should fulfill the pledges and promises that he makes to another person.

Imaan, the faraaidh and all the commands of Allaah are trusts that Allaah has placed in the custody of people. They should ensure that they fulfill these. Similarly, the trusts and secrets that people are entrusted with should also be duly kept with diligence.

Protection of the private parts Private parts here refers to the entire area between the navel and the knees for males, and the entire body for females, excluding the hands and feet. : This is of two categories. The first is that one safeguards them from being used for sinful purposes like adultery. The second is that a person ensures that no other person sees it. Allaah's curse is on the person who sees the private portion of another, as well as on the person who allows his/her private parts to be seen (this refers to those people who cannot see each other in terms of the shari'ah). Of course, others may see these at times of extreme necessity.

Lowering the gazes: This is also necessary so that a person does not inadvertently see the private parts of another or a person (who is not a mahram to them.) It is also necessary so that peoples' gazes do not fall on the things of this world, thereby enticing one towards these.

Restraining the hand: This refers to acquiring wealth by haraam means and oppressing people. A taabi'ee has mentioned, "Truthfulness is the beauty of the pious, while lying is the trait of the wretched."
Rasulullaah (sallAllaahu-alaihi-wasallam) has mentioned, "Backbiting means that you say something of your brother in his absence that he would not like." Someone asked, "What if the fact mentioned is really in him?" Rasulullaah (sallAllaahu-alaihi-wasallam) replied, "Then it is backbiting. If the fact is not in him, then it would constitute slander, which is worse than backbiting."

It has been mentioned that if it is said about someone, that his garb is too high or too low, then this will also be regarded as backbiting.

A short woman once came to Rasulullaah (sallAllaahu-alaihi-wasallam). After she left, Hadhrat A'isha (R.A) commented on her height. Rasulullaah (sallAllaahu-alaihi-wasallam) said, "Oh A'isha! This is backbiting because you have spoken ill of her."

THE STENCH OF BACKBITING CANNOT BE SMELT WHEN IT BECOMES HABITUAL.

Someone asked a saint, "Why is it that the stench of backbiting was smelt during the time of Rasulullaah (sallAllaahu-alaihi-wasallam), but is not evident today?" He replied, "Backbiting has become so common nowadays that it's stench has disappeared. The example is like how a toilet cleaner and a tanner become so accustomed to the stench of feces and raw leather, that they can eat quite comfortably in their environments whereas other will find it difficult to even stand there for a moment. This is how backbiting has taken vogue today."

A GIFT IN RETURN FOR EVIL.

Someone told Hadhrat Hasan Basri (R.A) that a certain person had gossiped about him. Hearing this, Hadhrat Hasan (R.A) sent a box of fresh dates to the person with the message, "I have come to learn that you have given me the rewards of your good actions. I have sent this small gift in appreciation. Please forgive me for not returning the favour in full."

A SAYING OF HADHRAT IBRAHEEM BIN ADHAM (R.A).

Hadhrat Ibraheem bin Adham (R.A) once invited some people for a meal. When they sat down to eat, they began speaking about someone. He told them, "People in the past used to eat the bread before their meat. However, you people have begun eating the meat before the bread (i.e. by backbiting). Rasulullaah (sallAllaahu-alaihi-wasallam) has assimilated backbiting as eating the flesh of a Muslim."

Hadhrat Ibraheem (R.A) once said, "Oh liars! You have been miserly towards your friends with regard to the world (i.e. you have not spent on their necessities). However, you have been extremely generous towards your enemies with regard to the Hereafter (i.e. by giving them all the rewards of your good actions when backbiting about them). You have no excuse for this miserliness, nor will you be praised for this generosity."

THREE THINGS DESTROY GOOD ACTIONS.

Rasulullaah (sallAllaahu-alaihi-wasallam) has mentioned that three things destroy the radiance and rewards of good actions.
(1) Lying,
(2) carrying tales and
(3) looking at the private parts of another person. These acts irrigate the roots of evil just like water irrigates the roots of trees.

THREE THINGS ARE DISTANT FROM MERCY.

Allaah's mercy is far from that gathering wherein three things are found (viz.)
(1) worldly talks,
(2) laughter and
(3) backbiting.

THREE QUALITIES OF THE PIOUS

Hadhrat Yahya bin Mu'aadh (R.A) says, "If you possess three qualities, you will be regarded as those who are righteous viz.

1. If you cannot be of benefit to anyone, then do not harm them.
2. If you cannot make anyone happy, then do not cause them sadness.
3. If you cannot speak good of anyone, then do not speak ill of them."

THE ATTITUDE OF THE ANGELS TOWARDS BACKBITING.

Hadhrat Mujaahid (R.A) said that whenever a person speaks well of another, the angels who remain with him say, "May Allaah keep the two of you alike." When he speaks ill of him, they say, "You have disclosed the faults of your brother. Look at yourself and thank Allaah that he has not disclosed your faults."

WORDS OF WISDOM DO 3 IF YOU CANNOT DO 3.

"Oh man! If you cannot do three things, then you should do another three.

1. If you cannot behave well towards anyone, then restrain yourself from behaving badly towards them.
2. If you cannot be of benefit to anyone, then guard them from your evil.
3. If you cannot fast, then refrain from eating their flesh (i.e. do not backbite).

WHO IS THE WORST PERSON?

Rasulullaah (sallAllaahu-alaihi-wasallam) once asked the Sahabahh (R.A), "Who is the worst person?" "Allaah and his Prophet (sallAllaahu-alaihi-wasallam) know best," was the reply. Rasulullaah (sallAllaahu-alaihi-wasallam) said, "The worst person is the one who carries tales, who tells everyone the same tale and speaks ill of others."

PUNISHMENT IN THE GRAVE FOR THOSE WHO CARRY TALES:- 3 CAUSES.

It has been mentioned that punishment in the grave is divided into three parts. A third is for backbiting, another third is for not being cautious when urinating, while the last third if for carrying tales.

CARRYING TALES AND SPREADING ANARCHY.

Hadhrat Hamaad bin Salma (R.A) narrates that a person once sold a slave, warning the buyer that the slave had the bad habit of carrying tales. Thinking nothing of the fault, he purchased the slave.

After a few days the slave approached his master's wife and told her that her husband no longer loved her and intended to marry someone else. She was extremely shocked, but he assured her of the fact. He then told her that he had a plan to secure his love for her. When she invoked him to inform her of his plan, he responded, "Shave off some hairs from below his beard while he sleeps. This is a tried and tested method."

The slave then approached the master and told him that his wife has fallen in love with another man and was waiting for an opportunity to murder him." When the master asked in surprise, "How is this possible?" The slave replied, "You may test her by pretending to sleep and then seeing what she will do."

That night the husband pretended to sleep. The wife was awaiting this opportunity and grabbed hold of a blade. The husband, being prepared, seized hold of the blade and killed her instead. When the relatives of the wife learnt of the murder, they had him executed. As a result the two families were divided.

THE PERSON WHO CARRIES TALES IS WORSE THAN THE DEVIL AND ONE WHO DABBLES IN BLACK MAGIC.

This is so because the person who carries tales causes as much harm in a minute than a person engaged in black magic does in a week. While shaytaan always does things indirectly and with deception, the tale carrier perpetrates his/her works openly.

SEVEN QUESTIONS.

Abu Abdullaah Al Qurashi (R.A) narrates that a person travelled seven hundred miles to ask a learned scholar seven questions viz.

1. What is heavier than the skies?
2. What is wider than the earth?
3. What is harder than a stone?
4. What burns more than fire?
5. What is colder than Zamhareer (a cold area of Jahannam)?
6. What is deeper than the oceans?
7. What is weaker than an orphan, yet more deadly than poison?

The replies were:

1. Slandering a chaste person is heavier than the skies.
2. The truth is wider than the earth.
3. The disbeliever's heart is harder than a stone.
4. Greed burns more than fire.
5. To be refused a request by a relative is colder than Zamhareer.

6. A content heart (of a patient person) is deeper than the oceans.
7. When the fabrication of a tale is exposed, it is more deadly than poison and the tale carrier then becomes weaker than an orphan and is humiliated.

A TALE CARRIER SHOULD NOT BE RELIED ON.

Hadhrat Hasan Basri (R.A) says that when a person carries a tale to you, then remember that he will certainly carry tales about you to others. Therefore, you should never believe anyone who speaks ill of others.

A person once spoke ill of another to Hadh.at Umar bin Abdul Aziz (R.A). The khalifa said, "If you are lying, then the following verse will apply to you viz. **'Oh you who believe, if a sinner brings any news to you, then verify it.'** However, if you are truthful, then the following verse will apply to you viz. **'The one who reviles and carries tales.'** (i.e. Your word cannot be relied on).

CARRYING TALES FORBIDS PRAYERS FROM BEING ACCEPTED.

Hadhrat Ka'b Ahbaar (R.A) says that a drought once afflicted the people of Hadhrat Moosa (A.S). Hadhrat Moosa (A.S) took the people to the plains to supplicate to Allaah, but to no avail. Hadhrat Moosa (A.S) supplicated, "Oh my Rabb! Your bondsmen have thrice beseeched You, but You have not responded."

Allaah told him, "Oh Moosa! There is a tale carrier amongst you, due to whom your du'as are not being accepted." Hadhrat Moosa (A.S) said, "Oh my Rabb! Inform us who this is so that we may be rid of him." Allaah replied, "How can We carry tales when We have forbidden the same? You should all repent collectively."

When they all repented, their du'a was accepted and the drought was lifted.

GEMS FROM THE LIPS OF THE PIOUS.

ȣ When someone informs you that another has been foul mouthing you, then remember that he (the informant) is actually the foul-mouthed one.

ȣ Hadhrat Wahab bin Munabbih (R.A) says, "When anyone sings any praises for you that are not applicable, then remember that he may someday speak such ills of you that also do not apply to you."

6 THINGS TO DO WHEN SPOKEN ILL OFF

ৎ Faqeeh Abul Laith Samarqandi (R.A) says that you should adopt the following six procedures when someone informs you that another has spoken ill of you.

1. Do not believe it (because the tale carrier is not to be trusted).
2. Forbid him from telling you (it is incumbent that the Muslim forbids evil).
3. Express your anger at him for the sake of Allaah (just like pleasure for Allaah's sake is encouraged, expressing anger for Allaah's sake is also commendable).
4. Do not entertain evil thoughts of the person being spoken about merely due to the information passed on by the tale carrier (because it is haraam to harbour ill thoughts about another Muslim).
5. Do not research the information given (because Allaah has forbidden spying on others).
6. Do not emulate the vile action that this tale carrier has perpetrated (i.e. do not relate this information to others).

SOME AHADEETH.

Rasulullaah (sallAllaahu-alaihi-wasallam) said, "The one who carries tales will not enter Jannah. The two-faced person will be in the worst condition on the Day of Judgement. He is the one who approaches one person with one face and another with another face." [Bukhari and Muslim]

Rasulullaah (sallAllaahu-alaihi-wasallam) has also mentioned that when a person tells lies, the angels run a mile from him due to the odour that emits from his mouth." [Tirmidhi]

Rasulullaah (sallAllaahu-alaihi-wasallam) has mentioned that the person who carries tales will have a tongue of fire on the Day of Qiyamah.

THE ABOMINATION OF JEALOUSY AND MALICE AND HOW TO REFRAIN FROM THESE.

Rasulullaah (sallAllaahu-alaihi-wasallam) has mentioned, "Malice and jealousy consume good actions just like fire consumes wood."

He has also mentioned that most people are involved in three evils (viz.)
(1) thinking ill of others,
(2) jealousy
(3) taking evil omens. When someone asked what the method was for abstaining from these three vices, Rasulullaah (sallAllaahu-alaihi-wasallam) replied,

1. Do not disclose your jealousy to anyone and do not speak ill of the person of whom you are jealous.
2. Do not think ill of anyone till you witness his evil yourself.
3. Do not take heed of any insects or crows on the roadside, nor of any twitches of your limbs (i.e. do not take any evil omens from these, whereby you would be reluctant to proceed further).

In this way, you will be saved from the evil of the above."

A SUPPLICATION.

Hadhrat Abdullah bin Abbaas (R.A) says that a person should recite the following du'a whenever he apprehends evil befalling him from certain quarters. The du'a is
He should pass by the cause while reciting this du'a. He will not be harmed by this.

THE EFFECT OF JEALOUSY FIRST BEFALLS THE JEALOUS PERSON :- 5 PUNISHMENTS OF JEALOUSY.

Faqeeh Abul Laith Samarqandi (R.A) has mentioned that jealousy is the most destructive of all sins because it causes the jealous person to be afflicted with five punishments before it can affect the person whom he is jealous of. These are:

1. An unending sorrow.
2. A calamity for which there is no reward.
3. He will be criticized from every angle without receiving any praise.
4. He will earn Allaah's wrath.
5. The door of guidance will be closed for him.

THE JEALOUS PERSON IS AN ENEMY OF ALLAAH'S BOUNTIES.

Rasulullaah (sallAllaahu-alaihi-wasallam) has mentioned, "Some people are enemies to Allaah's bounties." When someone enquired as to who they were, Rasulullaah (sallAllaahu-alaihi-wasallam) replied, "Those who are jealous of people who are enjoying good fortune."

THE RELIGIOUS SCHOLARS ARE MOST GUILTY OF JEALOUSY.

Hadhrat Maalik bin Dinaar (R.A) has said, "I will give precedence to the testimony of religious scholars over the testimony of all others, but not when it is given against other religious scholars. This is because I have found jealousy to be most prevalent amongst them."

SIX THINGS THAT WILL CONDEMN SIX PEOPLE TO JAHANNAM BEFORE RECKONING.

Rasulullaah (sallAllaahu-alaihi-wasallam) has mentioned that six people will be condemned to Jahannam on account of six evils even before reckoning commences. These are:

1. Leaders and rulers, due to their injustice.
2. The Arabs, due to tribal feudalism.

3. People in high positions, due to pride and arrogance.
4. Merchants, due to deception and misappropriation.
5. Villagers, due to their ignorance.
6. Religious scholars, due to jealousy. (This refers to those religious scholars who are jealous of each other due to their greed for the world. If a scholar is concerned of the Hereafter, he will not harbour any jealousy for another).

A SAYING:- 6 ADVICES.

Hadhrat Ahnaf bin Qais (R.A) says,

1. The jealous person can never enjoy any peace.
2. The miser can never fulfill any promises.
3. The small-hearted can never have any friends.
4. Self-respect cannot be earned by lying.
5. A traitor can never be trusted.
6. The ill-mannered person cannot have any love in him.

JEALOUSY CANNOT BE HARBOURED FOR ANYONE:-2 REASONS.

Hadhrat Muhammad bin Seereen (R.A) said, "I have never been jealous of anyone concerning worldly things because people are of two types. If he is pious and destined for Jannah, then why should I be jealous of him? If he is destined for Jahannam, then how can one be jealous of him?"

THE ADVICE OF RASULULLAAH (SALLIALLAAHU-ALAIHI-WASALLAM).

Hadhrat Anas bin Maalik (R.A) says that he remained in the service of Rasulullaah (sallAllaahu-alaihi-wasallam) from the age of eight.

Rasulullaah (sallAllaahu-alaihi-wasallam) first gave him the following advice, "Oh Anas! Perform wudhu well because it will bless your life and the protecting angels will love you. Be particular in taking a bath because impurities exist beneath every hair and sins are forgiven thereby. You must perform the mid morning salaah (Dhuha) because it is the salaah of those who repent. Also perform other salaah during the day and night, due to which the angels will pray for you. Carry out all the postures of salaah properly, for Allaah likes and accepts this type of salaah."

"Remain in the state of wudhu at all times, and you will not forget the kalimah at the time of death. Greet the inhabitants of your home when entering. This will create blessings in the home. Greet every Muslim you meet on the street. This will cause you to taste that sweetness of Imaan and you will be forgiven for the sinse committed while on that street. Do not harbor enmity or jealousy for a Muslim for even a moment. This is my way. Whoever will adopt my way has expressed love for me and whoever loves me will be with me in Jannah. Oh Anas! If you remember my advice and practice thereupon, death will be welcome to you and death will hold comfort for you."

THE JEALOUS PERSON OPPOSES ALLAAH IN 5 WAYS.

It has been mentioned that the jealous person opposes Allaah in five ways viz.

1. He detests every bounty that others receive from Allaah.
2. He expresses displeasure at the way in which Allaah distributes His bounties (he deems Allaah's distribution to be incorrect).
3. He is miserly with Allaah's grace (he does not want Allaah to bestow His grace upon whomsoever He pleases).
4. He humiliated Allaah's friends (the desire that another should be deprived of Allaah's bounty actually means that he desires the person to he humiliated).
5. He assists Allaah's enemy, Iblees (the purpose of Iblees's life is to deprive people of Allaah's grace).

PRIDE MEANS TO CONSIDER ONESELF AS BEING SUPERIOR AND TO LOOK DOWN ON OTHERS.

Hadhrat Hasan bin Ali (R.A) passed by some poor persons who were sitting on a shawl and eating from a piece of bread. Upon seeing him, they all invited him to partake of the meal. He alighted form his conveyance and joined them saying, "I do not like proud people." After eating with them, he took them all to his house and fed them whatever was available.

THREE PEOPLE ARE DESERVING OF PUNISHMENT.

Rasulullaah (sallAllaahu-alaihi-wasallam) has mentioned that Allaah will not speak to three persons on the Day of Qiyamah. He will not even look at them with mercy. However, He will subject them to a most excruciating punishment.

The first is the old man who fornicates. Although fornication is just as abominable in youth as it is in old age, it is much worse in old age because the old person is close to death and has begun to loose his carnal passions.

The second person is that king who lies. Lying is worse for a king because he has none to fear and cannot be forced into doing so.

The third person is a proud beggar. Pride is worse for a beggar because he has nothing to be proud of.

THE FIRST THREE PEOPLE TO ENTER JANNAH AND JAHANNAM.

Rasulullaah (sallAllaahu-alaihi-wasallam) has mentioned that he was shown the first three people to enter Jannah, as well as the first three to enter Jahannam. Those to be admitted first to Jannah shall be:

1. The martyr (who sacrificed his life in Allaah's path with sincerity).

2. The slave whose slavery did not prevent him from obeying Allaah. He obeyed his master without compromising on the commandments of Allaah.
3. The poor person who had children (he was physically weak, as well as handicapped by a lack of wealth and being a father to many children. However, he remained patient and grateful).

The first three to be entered into Jahannam shall be:

1. The ruler who continually oppressed his subjects.
2. The rich person who does not pay zakaah (it is futile to expect any charity from the person who cannot even pay his zakaah).
3. The proud beggar (being proud despite the impediments of destitution and poverty reveal a wretched and base personality).

ALLAAH DETESTS THREE PERSONS.

1. All sinners, especially those who are aged.
2. All misers, especially those who are wealthy.
3. All proud people, especially the proud beggar.

THE THREE PERSONS WHO ARE MOST BELOVED TO ALLAAH.

1. The abstinent, especially the abstinent youth.
2. The generous, especially the poor person who is generous.
3. The humble, especially a wealthy man who is humble.

THE REALITY OF PRIDE.

Rasulullaah (sallAllaahu-alaihi-wasallam) has mentioned that the person who has pride equivalent to a mustard seed will not enter Jannah. Someone asked, "I like my clothes and shoes to be nice and clean.

Is this also pride?" Rasulullaah (sallAllaahu-alaihi-wasallam) replied, "No. Allaah is beautiful and appreciates beauty. He wants to see the effects of His bounties on His bondsmen. Allaah dislikes a wealthy person from adopting the appearance of a poor person. Pride means that a person looks down upon others. The person who keeps his shoes in order, patches his clothing, and prostrates to Allaah is free from pride."

THE MOST DETESTABLE PERSON.

Hadhrat Moosa (A.S) once asked Allaah, "Which of your creation is most detestable in Your sight?" Allaah replied, "The person whose heart is filled with pride, whose tongue is harsh, whose conviction is weak and whose hands are miserly."

WORDS OF WISDOM.

"The fruit of patience is comfort and the fruit of humility is love. The pride of a Mu'min is his Rabb, his honour is his religion. On the other hand, the pride of the hypocrite is his lineage and his wealth is his honour."

ALLAAH DISLIKES STRUTTING.

Muhallab bin Mughiera, who was in the army of Hajaaj, once passed Mutarraf bin Abdullaah (R.A) strutting in elegant clothes. Mutarraf (R.A) told him, "Oh servant of Allaah! Allaah does not like this walk." Muhallab retorted, "Do you not know who I am?" Mutarraf (R.A) replied, "I know you very well. You were originally a drop of dirty fluid and will soon become a stinking corpse. At this point in time you are carrying a load of excrement with you." After hearing this Muhallab changed his walk.

GOOD CHARACTER MEANS TO BEHAVE HUMBLY TOWARDS THE HUMBLE AND BEHAVE PROUDLY WITH THE PROUD.

Rasulullaah (sallAllaahu-alaihi-wasallam) has mentioned, "Behave humbly towards the humble and proudly towards the proud. Your pride will be a cause of disgrace and humiliation to the proud people and it will be charity on your part."

THE HIGHEST FORM OF HUMILITY.

Hadhrat Umar (R.A) said, "The highest form of humility is that you greet every Muslim, are pleased with the worst place in a gathering and that you dislike being praised."

HUMILITY IS A TRAIT OF THE AMBIYAA (A.S), WHILE PRIDE IS THE TRAIT OF THE KUFFAAR.

Faqeeh Abul Laith Samarqandi (R.A) has mentioned that humility is the sterling quality of the Ambiyaa (A.S) and the pious. On the other hand, pride is the trait of the kuffar and people like Fir'oun. The humble and proud people are mentioned as follows in the Qur'aan:

- ⚥ **"The bondsmen of Rahmaan are those who walk upon the earth in humility."**
- ⚥ **"Oh Rasulullaah (sallAllaahu-alaihi-wasallam)! Behave humbly towards the believers."**

- ⚥ **"You [Oh Rasulullaah (sallAllaahu-alaihi-wasallam)] are a embodiment the most noble of character."**
- ⚥ **"When they are told that there is no deity besides Allaah they are arrogant."**
- ⚥ **"Verily those who do not worship Me due to their pride shall soon enter Jahannam in humiliation."**
- ⚥ **"Enter the doors of Jahannam, wherein you shall abide forever. Terrible inaction is the abode of the proud ones."**

৬ **"Undoubtedly Allaah does not like those who are proud."**

Humility is the most noble trait of good character. Rasulullaah (sallAllaahu-alaihi-wasallam) was so humble that he even rode a donkey and accepted the invitation of slaves.

THE HUMILITY OF HADHRAT IBN UMAR (R.A).

A visitor once came to Hadhrat Abdullah bin Umar (R.A) during the night while he was busy writing under a lantern. When the light of the lantern began to dwindle, the guest offered to fix it. Hadhrat Abdullah bin Umar (R.A) said, "It is contrary to good manners that a person takes service from his guest."

The guest then asked if he should awaken the slave. Hadhrat Abdullah bin Umar (R.A) replied, "No. He has just fallen off to sleep." Consequently, Hadhrat Abdullah bin Umar (R.A) got up himself and poured oil into the lantern. The guest then asked, "Why did you undergo such trouble when I was available?" Hadhrat Abdullah bin Umar (R.A) replied, "I was Ibn Umar then and I am Ibn Umar now as well. Pouring oil into the lantern did not diminish my rank in the least. In fact, Allaah loves those who are humble."

THE HUMILITY OF HADHRAT UMAR (R.A)

It is well known that when Hadhrat Umar (R.A) was travelling to Shaam, he took turns riding with his slave. While the one would ride the other would lead the animal by it's reins. On one occasion, Hadhrat Umar (R.A) placed his shoes beneath his arm so as to cross over some water. As they approached their destination, the governor, Hadhrat Abu Ubaidah (R.A) came to welcome them.

Seeing Hadhrat Umar (R.A) leading the animal, Hadhrat Abu Ubaidah (R.A), "Oh Ameerul Mu'mineen! The people have come out to meet you. It is not befitting for them to see you in this condition. Why do you not mount the animal? Hadhrat Umar (R.A) replied, "Allaah gave us honour by virtue of Islaam .Now I will not take heed to what people say. (I will not be unjust to this slave on account of what people have to say)."

THE HUMILITY OF HADHRAT SALMAAN FAARSI (R.A)

Hadhrat Salmaan Faarsi (R.A), after been appointed as governor of Madinah, was once walking through the marketplace. Mistaking him to be a slave, someone instructed him to carry a load. Hadhrat Salmaan (R.A) happily complied. As they were walking through the streets, people began to wonder in astonishment. Each one of them said, "May Allaah have mercy on you Oh Ameerul Mu'mineen! Allow us to carry the load." However, Hadhrat Salmaan (R.A) refused all of them and continued to carry the load.

When the person realized his error, he apologized for not recognizing the governor. Hadhrat Salmaan (R.A) said, "Do not worry about it. Just keep walking." The two eventually reached the person's house. The person was so embarrassed about his behaviour that he vowed never to employ the services of anyone.

THE HUMILITY OF HADHRAT ALI (R.A).

Hadhrat Ali (R.A) once purchased two garments from a shop and then asked his slave to first chose which of the two he liked best. The slave chose the better of the two for himself and Hadhrat Ali (R.A) happily wore the other. When Hadhrat Ali (R.A) noticed that the sleeves of his garment were too long, he asked for a scissors, cut the sleeves to size, and proceeded to deliver a sermon.

This was the behaviour of our predecessors. They were never fussy or demanding. On the other hand, we are totally different and cannot do without behaving querulously and demandingly.

RANKS ARE RAISED BY SPENDING IN CHARITY AND BY FORGIVING OTHERS WITHOUT 3 TRAITS GRANTS JANNAH.

Rasulullaah (sallAllaahu-alaihi-wasallam) has mentioned, "Wealth does not decrease when spent in charity (but rather increases). Forgiving the transgressions of others raises a person's ranks. If three traits are not within a person when he dies, he shall enter Jannah, viz. (1) pride, (2) betrayal and (3) debts."

Hadhrat Abu Umamah Baahili (R.A) narrates from Rasulullaah (sallAllaahu-alaihi-wasallam) that the person who controls his anger despite having the ability to vent it, will attain Allaah's complete pleasure on the Day of Judgement.

Allaah says the following in the Injeel: "Oh son of Aadam! Remember Me when you are angry and I will remember you when I am angry. Be happy with My assistance because it is better than yours."

IT IS INCORRECT TO PUNISH ANYONE TO GRATIFY ONESELF.

Hadhrat Umar bin Abdul Aziz (R.A) once had a drunkard arrested to face punishment. When the drunkard started to swear and abuse him, Hadhrat Umar bin Abdul Aziz (R.A) had him released. When someone enquired about this, Hadhrat Umar bin Abdul Aziz (R.A) replied, "I became angry when he began to swear me. If I had punished him in the condition of anger, the punishment would have been to appease myself. I do not like to have any Muslim punished merely to gratify myself."

ALLAAH LOVES THAT ONE FORGIVES ANOTHER.

A slave woman once dropped some gravy on the clothing of Hadhrat Maymoon bin Mihraan (R.A). When he became angry, the lady recited the following verse of the Qur'aan, **"Those who suppress their anger..."** His anger immediately abated.

Taking advantage of the situation, she recited the following part of the verse, viz. "...**and those who forgive people**..." He then told her that she was forgiven. Full exploiting the opportunity, she recited the concluding part of the verse, "...**and Allaah loves those who do good.**" Thereupon he said, "I free you for the pleasure of Allaah."

THE SWEETNESS OF IMAAN IS NOT TASTED WITHOUT THREE TRAITS.

Rasulullaah (sallAllaahu-alaihi-wasallam) said, "The person who does not possess three qualities cannot taste the sweetness of Imaan. (These are)
(1) Forbearance, by which the ignorance of the ignoramuses is rebutted.
(2) Taqwa (abstinence), by which haraam actions are avoided.
(3) Good character, by which one can associate with people."

AN INCIDENT OF HOW SHAYTAAN IS INFURIATED.

A saint possessed a horse, which he loved very much. One day, he noticed the horse standing on three legs. He asked his slave, "Who is responsible for this?" The slave admitted that it was him. The saint asked, "Why have you done this?" The slave replied, "I intended to aggravate you."

Thereupon the saint said, "Fine. I shall rather aggravate the one who instigated you to do this (i.e. shaytaan). Go! You are free, and you may have the horse as well."

AN ASTONISHING INCIDENT OF HOW SHAYTAAN DEVIATED PEOPLE :- 3 METHODS.

Shaytaan repeatedly tried to deviate a saint of the Bani Isra'eel. Once, when the saint came out of his house for some necessity, shaytaan attempted to aggravate him and entice his carnal passions. However, he failed each time. He even failed to threaten and frighten him. He caused a large boulder from a mountain to roll towards the saint, but that saint immediately engaged in dhikr, whereby the boulder was diverted in another direction.

Shaytaan even assumed the appearance of a lion and then a wolf to frighten the saint, but was unsuccessful. Shaytaan then assumed the appearance of a snake and coiled himself around the entire body of the saint as he performed salaah. He then placed his mouth wide open at the spot where the saint was to prostrate. However, this also had no effect on the saint.

Shaytaan finally admitted to the saint that he could not deviate him despite all his efforts. He added, "I have now decided to befriend you and have resolved never to attempt to mislead you again. Therefore, stretch out your hand to befriend me." The saint burst out, "You wretch! (i.e. This is your final plot to lead me astray. I do not require your friendship)." Shaytaan was now totally despondent and came face-to-face with the saint saying, "I wish to inform you how I mislead people." "Please do so," said the saint. Shaytaan said, "I employ three methods viz.
(1) Miserliness,
(2) jealousy and
(3) intoxication. When a person becomes miserly, he craves for accumulating wealth and does not want to spend on others. He is then engrossed in thoughts of how to usurp peoples' wealth and destroy the rights owed to them."
He continued to say, "The jealous person becomes a toy in our hands, just like a ball is in the hands of a child. Therefore do not concern ourselves with his acts of worship and spiritual exercises. Even though his du'as could resurrect the dead, we are still not overly concerned with him because we are able to destroy all his devotions and spiritual exercises by a single indication. When a person is intoxicated, we lead him by the ear like a goat and involve him in every type of sin with the greatest of ease."
Shaytaan also added that the person who is angry becomes like a ball in his hands. Shaytaan treats him just as a child who becomes happy when he tosses a ball around. Man should endeavour to restrain his anger so as not to become a toy for shaytaan.

HADHRAT MOOSA (A.S) AND IBLEES :- 3 CONDITIONS IN WHICH ONE SHOULD BE WARY OF SHAYTHAAN.

Iblees once came to Hadhrat Moosa (A.S) and told him, "You are the chosen messenger of Allaah and have been blessed with the privilege of speaking directly to Allaah. I wish to repent, so please intercede on my behalf before Allaah so that He may accept my repentance."

Hadhrat Moosa (A.S) was happy and thought that Iblees's repentance would put an end to sins. He therefore made wudhu, performed salaah and prayed to Allaah. Allaah told Hadhrat Moosa (A.S), "Iblees is lying. He merely wishes to deceive you. If he is really sincere, test him by telling him to prostrate before the grave of Hadhrat Aadam (A.S). If he does this, his repentance will be accepted."

Hadhrat Moosa (A.S) was extremely overjoyed, thinking that this was a very easy condition for Iblees to comply with. When Hadhrat Moosa (A.S) informed Iblees about the condition, Iblees became a whirlwind of fire and said, "I did not prostrate to him while he was alive, how can I prostrate to him when he is dead? Nevertheless, you have done me a good turn by interceding on my behalf. I shall therefore inform you of three conditions wherein you should be wary of me. (1) When man is angry, I run in his veins like his blood. (2) I incline the heart of the person fighting in jihaad towards his wife, children and wealth, thereby causing him to desert the battlefield **Shaytaan also attempts to dissuade the student of Deen in this manner. Strengthening one's resolve may combat him..** (3) When a strange man and woman are in isolation, I become the emissary between the two and incline each one towards the other. I remain engaged in this task until the two are tainted in sin."

THE ADVICE OF HADHRAT LUQMAAN (A.S):- RECOGNISE 3 ON 3 OCCASION.

Hadhrat Luqmaan (A.S) told his son, "Oh my son! You will recognize three types of persons on three occasions viz. (1) A forbearing person at the time of anger. (2) A brave person at the time of battle. (3) A friend at the time of poverty."

AN INCIDENT OF A TAABI'EE (R.A) :-
3 QUALITIES OF ONE WORTHY OF PRAISE
3 QUALITIES OF JAMATIES
3 ADVICES FROM ALLAAH .

When someone praised a certain Taabi'ee in his presence, he said, "Did you ever test me? Did you find me to be forbearing at the time of anger, displaying good character during a journey and trustworthy at the time of being trusted?" When the person replied in the negative, he said, "Then why have you praised me without first testing me? You should never praise anyone until you have tested them on these three accounts."

He then continued to say, "Three qualities are present in the people of Jannah, and these are exclusive to the noble people. (These are)
(1) Forgiving an oppressor,
(2) giving one who deprives you, and
(3) behaving well to someone who behaves ill towards you."

Allaah says, **"Adopt the habit of forgiveness, enjoin good and ignore the ignorant."** When this verse was revealed to Rasulullaah (sallAllaahu-alaihi-wasallam), he asked Hadhrat Jibreel (A.S) for an explanation thereto. Hadhrat Jibreel (A.S) enquired from Allaah, whereafter he informed Rasulullaah (sallAllaahu-alaihi-wasallam) saying, "Oh Muhammad (sallAllaahu-alaihi-wasallam)! Allaah commands that you join relationships with the relative who severs them, that you give to those who deprive you, and that forgive the one who oppresses you."

THE ASSISTANCE OF THE ANGELS UPON THE PATIENCE OF THE OPPRESSED: - 3 ACTS RESULT IN 3 OTHERS.

A person once swore Hadhrat Abu Bakr (R.A) in the presence of Rasulullaah (sallAllaahu-alaihi-wasallam). They both remained silent throughout. However, when the person stopped, Hadhrat Abu Bakr (R.A) replied to his abuse. Thereupon Rasulullaah (sallAllaahu-alaihi-wasallam) immediately got up and left.

When Hadhrat Abu Bakr (R.A) later asked him why he had done so, Rasulullaah (sallAllaahu-alaihi-wasallam) replied, "As long as you remained silent, an angel was replying to the abuse. However, when you began to reply, the angel left and shaytaan took his place. I therefore left. Three things are certain (viz.) (1) When an oppressed person forgives the oppressor, Allaah grants honour to the oppressed.
(2) The person who opens the door to begging due to greed for wealth will always remain a pauper.
(3) Allaah will increase the wealth of the person who continuously gives people gifts for Allaah's pleasure."

CONCISE WISDOMS.

Rasulullaah (sallAllaahu-alaihi-wasallam) has mentioned:

1. "Everything has a sterling factor, and the sterling factor of a gathering is that it is faced towards the Qibla and that the matters discussed are regarded a trust."
2. "Do not perform salaah behind people who are sleeping or talking."
3. "Kill a snake or a scorpion immediately upon sighting them even though you may be performing salaah."
4. "Do not hang curtains upon doors."
5. "The person who reads his brother's letter without permission has peeped into Jahannam."
6. "The person who wishes to be the greatest hero should trust only in Allaah."
7. "The person who wishes to be the most independent should have more reliance in what Allaah has than in what he possesses."
8. "The worst person is he who eats without feeding others and who beats his servant."

9. "Even worse than him is the person who detests people and is detested by people."

10. "Worse still is the person who does not catch one who is falling, who does not accept excuses and who does not forgive the shortcomings of others."

11. "Even worse is him from whom no good is expected and from whose evil others are not safe."

THE FOUR TYPES OF ASCETICISM.

1. Totally relying on Allaah in matters concerning the world and the Hereafter.

2. Praise and scorn are akin to him (i.e. he is not pleased with praise for him, nor affected by the scorn of others).

3. Having perfect sincerity in all actions.

4. Ignoring an oppressor, not getting angry at servants and slaves and being forbearing and patient.

THE 5 ADVICE OF HADHRAT ABU DARDAA (R.A).

When someone requested Hadhrat Abu Dardaa (R.A) for some useful advice, he said, "I am advising you with a few things that will guarantee a high position to whomsoever carries them out.

(1) Always eat halaal food.

(2) Beseech Allaah for the sustenance of each day.

(3) Always consider yourself amongst the dead.

(4) Hand over your honour to Allaah.

(5) Hasten to repent after every sin (even though the sin may seem small).

THE TEST OF STRENGTH.

Hadhrat Mujaahid (R.A) reports that Rasulullaah (sallAllaahu-alaihi-wasallam) once passed by some people who were competing with each other by lifting a weighty rock. Rasulullaah (sallAllaahu-alaihi-wasallam) said to them, "There is a heavier rock than this whereby you may able to test your strength."

When the people asked what this was, he replied, "For a brother to approach his brother in reconciliation after the two have been split over some issue and shaytaan has assumed control of both. (He then has to forgo the temporary 'honour' of this world and may even have to ask forgiveness. This he does for Allaah's pleasure)."

"Or," Rasulullaah (sallAllaahu-alaihi-wasallam) continued, "for a person to control his anger solely for Allaah's pleasure (even though he may be in a position to vent it)."

DO NOT CURSE AN OPPRESSOR.

Hadhrat Muhammad (sallAllaahu-alaihi-wasallam) said, "The person who curses an oppressor has grieved Muhammad (sallAllaahu-alaihi-wasallam) and pleased the accursed shaytaan. Whoever will forgive the oppressor has pleased Muhammad (sallAllaahu-alaihi-wasallam) and grieved the accursed shaytaan."

THE DEFINITION OF HUMANE BEHAVIOUR :-4 ADVICES,
3 BENEFITS OF PATIENCE, 3 HARMS OF HASTE

When someone asked Hadhrat Ahnaf bin Qais (R.A) as to what the definition of humane behaviour was, he replied,

"1.)Being humble, despite possessing wealth and riches.

2.) Forgiving, despite possessing the ability to avenge oneself.

3.) Assisting people without reminding them of your favour.

4.) Exercising patience at the time of anger instead of being hasty.

Patience has three benefits, while haste has three harms. The three benefits of patience are:
(1) The end result of patience leads to pleasure and happiness.
(2) People praise the patient person.
(3) Allaah will confer a bountiful reward to the patient person.

The three harms of haste are:
(1) It leads to regret and embarrassment.
(2) People curse the hasty person.
(3) He will receive a terrible punishment.

The beginning of forbearance is bitter, but it's end is sweeter than honey.

Hadhrat Hishaam bin Umar (R.A) has transmitted the hadith wherein Rasulullaah (sallAllaahu-alaihi-wasallam) has mentioned, "The expiation of slapping a slave is to set him free. The person who safeguards his tongue will be saved from punishment, and Allaah will accept the repentance of His slave. A Mu'min should entertain and honour his neighbours and guests. He should either speak good words or remain silent."

FOUR QUALITIES OF A BELIEVER.

Hadhrat Anas bin Maalik (R.A) reports that Rasulullaah (sallAllaahu-alaihi-wasallam) said, "Four qualities are only found in a Mu'min. (viz.) (1) Silence,
(2) humility,
(3) remembrance of Allaah,
(4) minimal evil."

A LOFTY POSITION OBTAINED BY 3 QUALITIES.

When someone asked the wise man, Hadhrat Luqmaan (A.S) as to how he attained his lofty position, he replied, "By
1.) truthfulness,
2.) trustworthiness and 3.) abstaining form futility."

THE STATEMENT OF FOUR KINGS.

Hadhrat Abu Bakr bin Ayyaash (R.A) says that four kings said the same thing in their respective times viz.

The Chosroe of Persia: "I have never regretted something that I have not spoken, but have mostly regretted what I have spoken."

The Emperor of China: "As long as I do not speak, I am that master of my words. However, after speaking them, you are the master."

The Caesar of Rome: "I am more capable of retracting what I have not spoken, than that which I have already spoken."

The Shah of India: "That person is astonishing who speaks in haste because his speech will cause him harm if it spreads and will be useless if it does not."

RECKONING IS EASIER IN THIS WORLD.

Every Muslim should reckon his own actions in this world because the reckoning of this world is much easier than that of the Hereafter. Controlling the tongue in this world is also much easier than the regret of the Hereafter.

THE SAINT THAT NEVER SPOKE A WRONG WORD FOR TWENTY YEARS.

A person narrates that he remained in the service of Hadhrat Rabee bin Khaitham (R.A) for a period of twenty years. He adds that during the entire period, the saint never said anything that was questionable.

However, when he was informed of the episode he looked towards the heavens and recited the following verse of the Qur'aan, **"Oh Allaah, the Creator of the heavens and the earth! Oh the Knower of the seen and the unseen. You judge between Your bondsmen with regard to the matters wherein they differ."**

He continues to narrate that he thought Hadhrat Rabee (R.A) would say something excessive upon the martyrdom of Hadhrat Husain (R.A).

SIX SIGNS OF AN IGNORAMUS.

A wise man once enumerated the following six traits of an ignorant person, viz.

1. He is infuriated without just cause (even animals and dead people make him angry).
2. He speaks without reason.
3. He gives without reason (without any benefit in this world or in the Hereafter).
4. He discloses secrets to all and sundry.
5. He trusts everyone.
6. He cannot differentiate between friend and foe (there are many evil people disguised as good men and a person living in this world should be able to recognize them for his own safety).

A STATEMENT OF HADHRAT ISA (A.S) 8 ADVICES.

Hadhrat Isa (A.S) said, "1. Every type of speech is futile except the dhikr of Allaah, and 2. silence is useless without meditation and deliberation. 3. All sights are useless unless they teach a lesson.
4. Blessed is the person whose speech is the dhikr of Allaah, 5. whose silence is in contemplation of the Hereafter, 6. and whose sightseeing is with a lesson. 7. A believer talks less and does more, 8. while a hypocrite talks more and does less."

THE ABOMINATION OF EXCESSIVE LAUGHTER AND 2 HABITS OF THE IGNORANT.

Hadhrat Isa (A.S) addressed his disciples saying, "Oh you, who are the salt of the earth! You should never be corrupted. Every spoilt thing can be cured with salt, but there is nothing to cure salt that has spoilt. You should not accept any remuneration for your teaching, save that which you have given to me. Remember, you have two habits of the ignorant, (1) laughing loudly and (2) sleeping during the early hours of the morning (if you had not remained awake during the night)."

Explanation: Hadhrat Isa (A.S) refers to the learned scholars as the salt of the earth because they need to rectify the masses who have gone astray. However, if they have to succumb to the pleasures of this world to their carnal desires and to the lethal traits of jealousy and hatred, none can correct them. The masses will then be left without leadership.

The Ambiyaa (A.S) propagated and taught solely for Allaah's pleasure and never demanded remuneration. Hadhrat Isa (A.S) therefore advised his disciples to do the same. Allaah says in the Qur'aan, **"Say, 'I do ask you for any remuneration for this. My remuneration is Allaah's responsibility."**

The ulema, being the heirs of the Ambiyaa (A.S), should also act likewise. Although it is perfectly permissible to accept payment for imparting the knowledge of Deen, none can deny the superior stance of teaching solely for Allaah's pleasure and, at the same time, adopting some other means of earning a livelihood. This was the method adopted by the early ulema. The latter scholars have permitted the acceptance of a salary for teaching due to pressing circumstances.

Laughing loudly (guffawing) is Makrooh and the habit of ignorant people, just as it is to sleep in the beginning of the day (unless one did not sleep at night).

THE ADVICE OF RASULULLAAH (sallAllaahu-alaihi-wasallam).

Rasulullaah (sallAllaahu-alaihi-wasallam) said, "It is foolish to sleep during the opening hours of the day, a good habit to sleep in the afternoons, and an act of ignorance to sleep during the last portion."

Rasulullaah (sallAllaahu-alaihi-wasallam) was passing by a Masjid when he noticed some people talking of worldly matters and laughing loudly. After greeting them, he said, "Think of death." He then proceeded. He later passed by again and noticed that they were still at it. He told them, "By Allaah! If you people knew what I do, you would laugh less and cry more."

It so happened that Rasulullaah (sallAllaahu-alaihi-wasallam) again passed by the same group for a third time. Noticing that they had not changed their behaviour, he said, "This Deen had begun as a stranger and will again be a stranger, so glad tidings be for the strangers." When he was asked who he was referring to by the "strangers, Rasulullaah (sallAllaahu-alaihi-wasallam) said, "Those who remain steadfast upon the Deen when the ummah has become corrupt."

FOUR ADVICE OF HADHRAT KHIDR (A.S).

When Hadhrat Moosa (A.S) was leaving Hadhrat Khidr (A.S), he asked him for some parting advice. Hadhrat Khidr (A.S) said, "Oh Moosa!
1. Do not beg importunately before anyone,
2. do not go anywhere without reason,
3. do not laugh except for something extremely surprising and
4. never remind any person of his folly because then people will remind you of yours."

A PERSON SHOULD NEVER LAUGH LOUDLY.

Hadhrat Awf bin Abdillah (R.A) narrates that Rasuluilaah (sallAllaahu-alaihi-wasallam) never laughed loudly, but would simply smile. He would also never look a person straight in the eye.

A SAYING OF HADHRAT HASAN BASRI (R.A).

"The person who laughs loudly is surprising, since Jahannam is behind him. Surprising is the person who is happy whereas death is ahead of him."

Once, upon seeing a youngster laughing, he said, "Oh son! Have you already crossed the bridge of Siraat? Have you already come to know that you are bound for Jannah and will be saved from Jahannam?" When the boy replied in the negative, Hadhrat Hasan (R.A) said, "Then why are you laughing?" It is reported that the boy was never seen laughing again.

FOUR FACTORS PREVENT LAUGHTER.

Hadhrat Yahya bin Mu'aadh Raazi (R.A)mentioned that four factors prevent man from laughing and being happy. These are:
(1) Concern for the Hereafter,
(2) involvement in earning,
(3) grief over one's sins, and
(4) being afflicted by calamities.

THREE THINGS HARDEN THE HEART.

1. Laughing without reason.
2. Eating without being hungry.
3. Talking without reason.

LAUGHING AND MAKING OTHERS LAUGH LEADS TO DESTRUCTION.

Rasulullaah (sallAllaahu-alaihi-wasallam) has mentioned, "That person is destroyed who invents lies to make people laugh."

Hadhrat Ibrahaam Nakha'ee (R.A) has mentioned, "When a person says something to make people laugh, the hearts of the speaker and the listeners become hard. When a person says something to please Allaah, then Allaah's mercy descends upon the gathering, causing all to benefit."

BENEFICIAL ADVICE,
5 ADVICES OF RASULULLAAH (S.A.W).

Rasulullaah (sallAllaahu-alaihi-wasallam) told Hadhrat Abu Huraira (R.A), "Oh Abu Hurairah!
1. Adopt piety, you will be recorded as those who worship Allaah abundantly.
2. Be content, and you will be deemed as a grateful person.
3. You will be a Mu'min if you like for others what you like for yourself.
4. You will be a Muslim if you behave well towards your neighbours.
5. Laugh less because excessive laughter kills the heart."

8 ADVICES OF HADHRAT UMAR (R.A)

Hadhrat Umar (R.A) told Hadhrat Ahnaf bin Qais (R.A), "
1. The awe shown to a person will be reduced by excessive laughter. 2. The person who jokes becomes humiliated, and a
3. person becomes renowned for that activity wherein he invests most of his time.
4. The person who talks excessively becomes disgraced and shame faced.
5. The person who loses face loses respect.
6. The person who is immmodest loses fear of Allaah, and
7. the heart of one who loses Allaah's fear eventually dies.
8. Only Jahannam is befitting for the person whose heart has died."

8 HARMS OF LAUGHING EXCESSIVELY

Imaam Abu Laith (R.A) says, "Abstain from laughing excessively and loudly. Eight harms come to the person who laughs excessively. These are:

1. The ulema and wise men scorn such a person.
2. The ignorant and foolish people become bold before him.
3. Laughing increases his ignorance (if he is ignorant) and reduces his knowledge (if he is learned). {Rasulullaah (sallAllaahu-alaihi-wasallam) has mentioned that one portion of knowledge is reduced when a learned person laughs}
4. Laughter causes one to forget his sins.
5. Laughter makes one bold enough to continue sinning.
6. Excessive laughter causes a person to forget death.
7. When others laugh because of him, all their resultant sins accrue to him.
8. Laughing in this world leads to excessive weeping in the Hereafter.

May Allaah save us all from excessive laughter and from all sins. Ameen.

****
****

1421 / 2001

HEROIC DEED OF MUSLIM WOMEN

Daughters of the Holy Prophet

S.M. Madni Abbasi

HOW TO SAY YOUR PRAYERS

A Comprehensive Guidance to Salat-e-Offering

BY :
MAULANA MOHD. M. F. USMANI

LEARN ISLAM SERIES

KITAABUT TAHAARAH

(THE BOOK OF PURIFICATION)

KITAB-US-SALAAT
(MUSLIM PRAYER BOOK)

Kitab-ul-Imaan

SALAH

ASHAB-AL-KAHF The Stunning Story of the Sleepers

Mohamad Yasin Owadally

HARUT AND MARUT

The Fallen Angels

MOHAMMAD YASIN OWADALLY

QITMIR, THE PEACOCK THE BLESSED DOG AND OTHER STORIES

M. Yasin Owadally

QAF

THE MYSTERIOUS, EMERALD MOUNTAIN DECODED

A weird world within this world separating the seen from the unseen with strange creatures, cities and events.

MOHAMAD YASIN OWADALLY

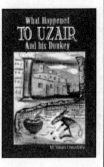

What Happened TO UZAIR And his Donkey

M. Yasin Owadally

THE CITY OF GIANTS

Mohamed Yasin Owadally

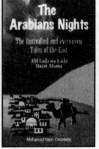

The Arabians Nights

The Unrivalled and evergreen Tales of the East

Alif Laila wa Laila Hazar Afsana

Mohamad Yasin Owadally

THE STORY OF YAJUJ-WA-MAJUJ AND THE WALL

Mohamad Yasin Owadally

The Fantastic Adventures of HATIM TAI

The marvellous but perilous adventures of Hatim Tai in the Quest of seven answers from the Arabian and Persian Literature

Mohamed Yasin Owadally

The Ethical Philosophy of Al-Ghazzali

Prof. M. Umaruddin

JALALUDDIN RUMI

PHILOSOPHY a critique

MAULANA ASHRAF ALI THANVI

Prof. Aftrud Al-Khwaja

THE MASTERPIECE OF SUFISM 1

Sūfism
– The Mystical Doctrines and The Idea Of Personality
W. Seddiket & R.A. Nicholson

THE MASTERPIECE OF SUFISM 2

Studies in Islamic Mysticism
R.A. Nicholson

THE MASTERPIECE OF SUFISM 3

Islamic Sūfism
S. Iqbal Ali Shah

THE MASTERPIECE OF SUFISM 4

Mystic Tendencies in Islam
M.M. Zahur-ud-Din Ahmad

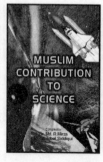

MUSLIM CONTRIBUTION TO SCIENCE

Compiled by Dr. Md. R.Mirza, Iqbal Siddiqui

Tuh-fatul Ikhwaan

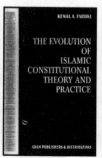

KEMAL A. FARUKI

THE EVOLUTION OF ISLAMIC CONSTITUTIONAL THEORY AND PRACTICE

ADAM PUBLISHERS & DISTRIBUTORS

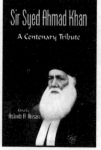

Sir Syed Ahmad Khan
A Centenary Tribute

Asloob A. Ansari

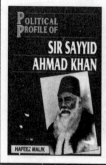

POLITICAL PROFILE OF SIR SAYYID AHMAD KHAN

HAFEEZ MALIK

A HISTORY OF URDU LITERATURE

Ram Babu Saxena

MODERN URDU POETS

YUNUS AHMAR

Social Philosophy of Sir MUHAMMAD IQBAL

Dr. Abdul Aleem Hilal

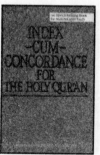

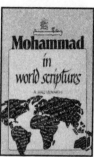
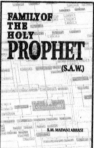

SAYYID JAMAL AL-DIN
AL-AFGHANI
and
THE WEST

SHEIKH JAMEIL ALI

MUHAMMAD
and his
CONSTITUTIONAL
CHARTER

Brig. Gulzar Ahmed

The Life of
MUHAMMAD

A.H. SIDDIQUI

300

Authenticated
Miracles of
MUHAMMAD

BADR AZIMABADI

Mercy for
Mankind
Rahmtul-lil-Alameen

Qazi Sulaiman Mansoorpuri

The Companions of
The Holy
Prophet

RAFI AHMAD FIDAI
N.M. SHAIKH

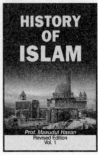

HISTORY
OF
ISLAM

Prof. Masudul Hasan
Revised Edition
Vol. 1

ISLAM
UNIVERSAL
RELIGION

PROF. Z. AHMED

DO YOU KNOW
WHAT ISLAM IS

Maulana M. Manzoor Nomani

A
COMPREHENSIVE
GUIDE BOOK
OF
ISLAM

ALTAF A. KHERI

GREAT
PERSONALITIES
IN ISLAM

BADR AZIMABADI

History Testifies
to the Infallibility
of the Qur'an
Early History of
the Children of Israel

GOLDEN TALES
OF
THE PROPHET

ABDUL-FATTAH JAMIL BARI

Duraid & Fait Faroohi

THE
QUR'ANIC
CONCEPT
OF HISTORY

MAZHERUDDIN SIDDIQI

A Literary History
Of
The Arabs

R.A. NICHOLSON

WOMEN IN ISLAM
M. Muzheruddin Siddiqi

SOLUTION TO YOUTH'S PROBLEM
ASGHAR ALI CHOWDHRY

WOMAN AND ISLAMIC LAW
Safia Iqbal

Women's Rights in Islam
MUHAMMAD SHARIF CHAUDHRY

The Concept of Family in Islam
A.D. Ajijola

Islamic Principles on Family Planning
Mufti Allie Haroun Sheik

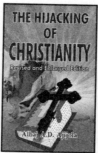

THE HIJACKING OF CHRISTIANITY
Revised and Enlarged Edition
Alhaj A.D. Ajijola

THE MYTH OF THE CROSS
A.D. AJIJOLA

ISLAM THE FINAL CHOICE
BADAR AZIMABADI

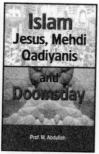

Islam Jesus, Mehdi Qadiyanis and Doomsday
Prof. M. Abdullah

COMPARATIVE STUDY OF CHRISTIANITY & ISLAM
Sh. Mohammad Ashraf

WEST VIS ISLAM
Syed A. A. Maududi

The Choice Islam and Christianity
Prof. M. Abdullah

UNSEEN GOD
Dr. N. K. Singh

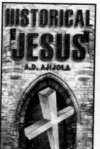

HISTORICAL 'JESUS'
A.D. AJIJOLA

Islamic Tasawwuf Shariah Tariqah
Prof. Mohammad Abdullah

طبِ نبوی
Prophetic Way of Treatment

Badr Azimabadi

Chronology of
The Prophetic Events

Fazlur Rehman Shaikh

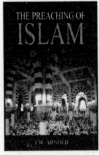

THE PREACHING OF
ISLAM

T.W. ARNOLD

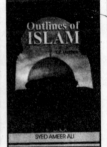

Outlines of ISLAM
T.P. Hughes

SYED AMEER ALI

THE SOUL
Its where about in the light of Qur'an & Hadith

الروح

Allama Ibn Qayyem

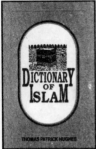

DICTIONARY OF ISLAM

THOMAS PATRICK HUGHES

ANECDOTES FROM
ISLAM

EBRAHIM KHAN

Beha Ed-Din

THE LIFE OF
SALADIN
(1137-1193 A.D.)

Contemporary
Muslim World

Dr. Afzal Iqbal

Islam and Muslims in South Asia:
Historical Perspective

Prof. Iqtidar Husain Siddiqui

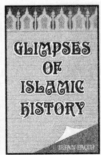

GLIMPSES OF ISLAMIC HISTORY

IRFAN FAQIH

HISTORY OF
MUSLIM SPAIN

The **Caliphate**

Sir Thomas W. Arnold

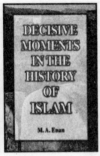

DECISIVE MOMENTS IN THE HISTORY OF ISLAM

M. A. Enan

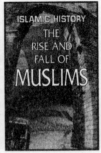

ISLAMIC HISTORY
THE RISE AND FALL OF
MUSLIMS

CONTRIBUTION AND
CULTURAL HISTORY OF
ISLAM